STEP-BY-STEP

COMPLETE
Italian
COOKING

·PARRAGON·

STEP-BY-STEP
COMPLETE
Italian
COOKING

ROSEMARY WADEY

PAMELA WESTLAND

WENDY LEE

First published in Great Britain in 1995 by
Parragon Book Service Ltd
Unit 13–17
Avonbridge Trading Estate
Atlantic Road
Avonmouth
Bristol BS11 9QD

ISBN 0-7525-0121-6

Printed in Italy

Acknowledgements:
Art Direction: Ron Samuels
Editors: Beverly LeBlanc, Diana Vowles
Page Design: Pedro & Frances Prá-Lopez/Kingfisher Design
Jacket Design: Somewhere Creative
Photography: Martin Brigdale, Amanda Heywood, Joff Lee
Home Economists: Jill Eggleton, Carole Handslip, Wendy Lee
Styling: John Lee Studios, Marian Price, Helen Trent
Step-by-Step Photography Section 1: Karl Adamson
Step-by-Step Home Economist Section 1: Joanna Craig

Photographs on pages 12, 28, 44, 54, 68, 84, 98, 118, 138, 154,
166, 182, 198 and 212 reproduced by permission of ZEFA Picture
Library (UK) Ltd.

Material contained in this book has previously appeared in
Italian Regional Cooking, Pasta Dishes and *Pizzas*.

Note:
*Cup measurements in this book are for American cups. Tablespoons are
assumed to be 15ml. Unless otherwise stated, milk is assumed to be full-
fat, eggs are standard size 2 and pepper is freshly ground black pepper.*

Contents

COMPLETE

Italian

COOKING

With its exotic range of mouthwatering yet
healthy and nutritious dishes, Italian
cooking appeals to just about everyone. The
various regional cuisines all have something
special to offer, from quick and easy pasta
dishes to more ambitious delicacies such as
Saltimbocca and Tiramisu.

The warmth and vitality for which Italy is
renowned is reflected in the country's
cuisine, and this comprehensive book will
enable you to sample tasty dishes from all
over Italy. Over the following pages you will
find dishes with irresistible flavours and
aromas to tempt your taste buds and
encourage you to enter the wonderful
world of Italian cooking.

ANTIPASTI & SOUPS

•

PASTA & PIZZA

•

FISH & SHELLFISH

•

MEAT & POULTRY

•

DESSERTS

1

ITALIAN
REGIONAL
COOKING

CHAPTER ONE

Antipasti & Soups

The word antipasto (plural antipasti) means 'before the main course' and what is served may be simple and inexpensive or highly elaborate. Antipasti usually come in three categories: meat, fish and vegetables. There are many varieties of cold meats, including ham, invariably sliced paper-thin. The best known is Parma ham (prosciutto), but there are many others, especially from the mountain areas, all of which can be served with slices of melon and figs. Numerous vegetables feature in antipasto dishes, served raw or marinated, deep-fried or pickled, with and without dressings. All varieties of fish are combined for the *antipasti di pesce*, including inkfish, octopus and cuttlefish. Huge prawns (shrimp) and mussels appear in various guises and fresh sardines are always popular.

Soups too are a very important part of the Italian cuisine. They vary in consistency from very thin to virtually knife and fork soups. Minestrone is known world-wide, but the best-known version probably came from Milan; however, all kinds are full of vegetables, often with pasta or rice plus beans, and are delicious and satisfying. Fish soups abound in one guise or another, and most of these are village specialities, so the variety is unlimited. Many of these soups constitute a whole meal, particularly those with a large proportion of beans, or with lightly toasted slices of bread added to the bowl.

Opposite: The Grand Canal, Venice. With its close proximity to the sea, fish and seafood dishes are found in abundance around Venice and the north-east corner of Italy.

STEP 1

STEP 1

STEP 4

STEP 5

FISH SOUP

All over Italy the selection of fish is enormous. There are many varieties of fish soup, some including shellfish. You will find cream soups, thin soups and thick soups: this one, from Tuscany, is like a chowder.

SERVES 4–6

1 kg/2 lb assorted prepared fish (including mixed fish fillets, squid, etc.)
2 onions, sliced thinly
few sprigs fresh flat-leaf parsley
2 bay leaves
2 celery sticks, sliced thinly
150 ml/¼ pint/⅔ cup white wine
1 litre/1¾ pints/4½ cups water
2 tbsp olive oil
1 garlic clove, crushed
1 carrot, chopped finely
425 g/15 oz can peeled tomatoes, puréed
2 potatoes, peeled and chopped
1 tbsp tomato purée (paste)
1 tsp freshly chopped oregano or ½ tsp dried oregano
350 g/12 oz fresh mussels
175 g/6 oz peeled prawns (shrimp)
2 tbsp chopped fresh parsley
salt and pepper
crusty bread, to serve

1 Cut the cleaned and prepared fish into slices or cubes and put into a large saucepan with 1 sliced onion, the parsley sprigs and bay leaves, 1 sliced celery stick, the wine and the water. Bring to the boil, cover and simmer for about 25 minutes.

2 Strain the fish stock and discard the vegetables and herbs. Skin the fish, remove any bones and reserve.

3 Heat the oil in a pan, finely chop the remaining onion and fry with the garlic, carrot and remaining celery until soft but not coloured. Add the puréed canned tomatoes, potatoes, tomato purée (paste), oregano, reserved stock and seasonings. Bring to the boil and simmer for about 15 minutes or until the potatoes are almost tender.

4 Meanwhile, thoroughly scrub the mussels. Add to the pan with the prawns (shrimp) and simmer for about 5 minutes or until the mussels have opened (discard any that stay closed).

5 Add the fish to the soup with the chopped parsley, bring back to the boil and simmer for 5 minutes. Adjust the seasoning.

6 Serve the soup in warmed bowls with chunks of fresh crusty bread, or put a toasted slice of crusty bread in the base of each bowl before adding the soup. If possible, remove a few half shells from the mussels before serving.

STEP 1

STEP 2

STEP 4

STEP 5

RED BEAN SOUP

Beans feature widely in Italian soups, making them hearty and tasty. If you prefer you can use other varieties of beans in this soup, which is from Tuscany and Lazio.

SERVES 4–6

175 g/6 oz/scant 1 cup dried red kidney beans, soaked overnight
1.7 litres/3 pints/7¹/₂ cups water
1 large ham bone or bacon knuckle
2 carrots, chopped
1 large onion, chopped
2 celery sticks, sliced thinly
1 leek, trimmed, washed and sliced
1–2 bay leaves
2 tbsp olive oil
2–3 tomatoes, peeled and chopped
1 garlic clove, crushed
1 tbsp tomato purée (paste)
60 g/2 oz/4 tbsp arborio or other short-grain rice
125–175 g/4–6 oz green cabbage, shredded finely
salt and pepper

1 Drain the beans and put into a saucepan with enough water to cover. Bring to the boil and boil hard for 15 minutes, then reduce the heat and simmer for 45 minutes. (The boiling is essential with kidney beans to kill naturally occurring toxins.) Drain.

2 Put the beans into a clean saucepan with the measured amount of water, ham bone or knuckle, carrots, onion, celery, leek, bay leaves and olive oil. Bring to the boil, cover and simmer for 1 hour or until the beans are very tender.

3 Discard the bay leaves and bone, reserving any ham pieces from the bone. Remove a small cupful of the beans and reserve. Purée or liquidize the soup in a food processor or blender and return it to a clean pan.

4 Add the tomatoes, garlic, tomato purée (paste), rice and plenty of seasoning. Bring back to the boil and simmer for about 15 minutes or until the rice is tender.

5 Add the cabbage and reserved beans and ham and continue to simmer for 5 minutes. Adjust the seasoning and serve very hot. If liked, a piece of toasted crusty bread may be put in the base of each soup bowl before ladling in the soup. If the soup is too thick, add a little boiling water or stock.

MINESTRONE WITH PESTO

One of the many versions of minestrone, which is always full of a variety of vegetables, pasta and rice and often includes beans. This soup is flavoured with pesto sauce, so often added to pasta dishes.

STEP 1

SERVES 6

175 g/6 oz/scant 1 cup dried cannellini beans, soaked overnight
2.5 litres/4 pints/10 cups water or stock
1 large onion, chopped
1 leek, trimmed, washed and sliced thinly
2 celery sticks, sliced very thinly
2 carrots, chopped
3 tbsp olive oil
2 tomatoes, peeled and chopped roughly
1 courgette (zucchini), trimmed and sliced thinly
2 potatoes, peeled and diced
90 g/3 oz elbow macaroni (or other small macaroni)
salt and pepper
4–6 tbsp grated Parmesan

PESTO:
2 tbsp pine kernels (nuts)
5 tbsp olive oil
2 bunches fresh basil, stalks removed
4–6 garlic cloves, crushed
90 g/3 oz/¾ cup Pecorino or Parmesan cheese, grated
salt and pepper

1 Drain the beans, rinse and place in a saucepan with the measured water or stock. Bring to the boil, cover and simmer gently for 1 hour.

2 Add the onion, leek, celery, carrots, and oil. Cover and simmer for 4–5 minutes.

3 Add the tomatoes, courgette (zucchini), potatoes and macaroni and seasoning. Cover again and continue to simmer for about 30 minutes or until the beans are very tender.

4 Meanwhile, make the pesto. Fry the pine kernels (nuts) in 1 tablespoon of the oil until pale brown, then drain. Put the basil into a food processor or blender with the pine kernels (nuts) and garlic. Process until finely chopped. Gradually add the oil until smooth. Turn into a bowl, add the cheese and seasoning and mix thoroughly.

5 Stir 1½ tablespoons of the pesto into the soup until well blended, simmer for a further 5 minutes and adjust the seasoning. Serve very hot, sprinkled with the cheese.

PESTO

Store in an airtight container for up to a week in the refrigerator; or freeze (without adding the cheese) for several months.

STEP 2

STEP 3

STEP 5

AUBERGINE (EGGPLANT) SALAD

*A first course with a difference from Sicily. This has a real bite, both
from the sweet-sour sauce, with its surprising flavouring of chocolate,
and from the texture of the celery.*

STEP 1

STEP 3

STEP 4

STEP 5

SERVES 4

2 large aubergines (eggplants), about
    1 kg/2 lb
salt
6 tbsp olive oil
1 small onion, peeled and chopped finely
2 garlic cloves, crushed
6–8 celery sticks
2 tbsp capers
12–16 green olives, pitted and sliced
2 tbsp pine kernels (nuts)
30 g/1 oz bitter or dark chocolate, grated
4 tbsp wine vinegar
1 tbsp brown sugar
salt and pepper
2 hard-boiled (hard-cooked) eggs, sliced, to
    serve
celery leaves or endive (chicory), to garnish

1 Cut the aubergines (eggplants) into
2.5 cm/1 inch cubes and sprinkle
liberally with 2–3 tablespoons salt. Leave
to stand for an hour, to extract the bitter
juices, then rinse off the salt thoroughly
under cold water, drain and dry on paper
towels.

2 Heat most of the oil in a frying pan
(skillet) and fry the aubergines
(eggplants) until golden brown. Drain on
paper towels, then transfer to a bowl.

3 Add the onion and garlic to the pan
with the remaining oil and fry very
gently until just soft. Cut the celery into
1 cm/½ inch slices, add to the pan and fry
for a few minutes, stirring frequently,
until lightly coloured but still crisp.

4 Add the celery to the aubergines
(eggplants) with the capers, olives
and pine kernels (nuts) and mix lightly.

5 Stir the chocolate and vinegar into
the residue in the pan with the
sugar. Heat gently until melted, then
bring up to the boil. Season with a little
salt and plenty of freshly ground black
pepper and pour over the salad. Mix
lightly, cover, leave until cold and then
chill thoroughly.

6 Serve with sliced hard-boiled
(hard-cooked) eggs and garnish
with celery leaves or endive (chicory).

NOTE

This salad will keep for several days in a
covered container in the refrigerator.
Chopped green tomatoes may also be
added to this salad, in season.

MOZZARELLA IN CAROZZA

A delicious way of serving cheese, a speciality of Campania and the Abruzzi. The cheese stretches out into melted strings as you cut it to eat. Some versions have Parma ham (prosciutto) added, too.

STEP 1

SERVES 4

200 g/7 oz Mozzarella cheese
4 slices Parma ham (prosciutto), about
 90 g/3 oz
8 slices white bread, preferably 2 days old,
 crusts removed
a little butter for spreading
2–3 eggs
3 tbsp milk
vegetable oil for deep-frying
salt and pepper
flat-leaf parsley, to garnish (optional)

TOMATO AND (BELL) PEPPER SAUCE:
1 onion, chopped
2 garlic cloves, crushed
3 tbsp olive oil
1 red (bell) pepper, cored, deseeded and
 chopped
425 g/15 oz can peeled tomatoes
2 tbsp tomato purée (paste)
3 tbsp water
1 tbsp lemon juice

1 First make the sauce: fry the onion and garlic in the oil until soft. Add the (bell) pepper and continue to cook for a few minutes. Add the tomatoes, tomato purée (paste), water, lemon juice and seasoning. Bring up to the boil, cover and simmer for 10–15 minutes or until

tender. Cool the sauce a little, then purée or liquidize until smooth and return to a clean pan.

2 Cut the Mozzarella into 4 slices so they are as large as possible; if the cheese is square, cut it into 8 slices. Trim the ham slices to the same size as the cheese.

3 Lightly butter the bread and use the cheese and ham to make 4 sandwiches, pressing the edges well together. If liked, they may be cut in half at this stage. Chill.

4 Lightly beat the eggs with the milk and seasoning in a shallow dish.

5 Carefully dip the sandwiches in the egg mixture until well coated all over, and if possible leave to soak for a few minutes.

6 Heat the oil in a large pan until it just begins to smoke, or until a cube of bread browns in about 30 seconds. Fry the sandwiches in batches until golden brown on both sides. Drain on paper towels and keep warm. Serve the sandwiches hot, with the reheated sauce, and garnished with parsley.

STEP 3

STEP 5

STEP 6

STEP 1

STEP 2

STEP 3

STEP 6

CROSTINI ALLA FIORENTINA

*A coarse pâté from Tuscany which can be served as a casual first course
or simply spread on small pieces of crusty fried bread (crostini) to serve
as an appetizer with drinks.*

SERVES 4

3 tbsp olive oil
1 onion, chopped
1 celery stick, chopped
1 carrot, chopped
1–2 garlic cloves, crushed
125 g/4 oz chicken livers
125 g/4 oz calf's, lamb's or pig's liver
150 ml/¼ pint/⅔ cup red wine
1 tbsp tomato purée (paste)
2 tbsp chopped fresh flat-leaf parsley
3–4 canned anchovy fillets, chopped finely
2 tbsp stock or water
30–45 g/1–1½ oz/2–3 tbsp butter
1 tbsp capers
salt and pepper
small pieces of fried crusty bread (see
   right)
chopped fresh parsley, to garnish

1 Heat the oil in a pan, add the
onion, celery, carrot and garlic
and cook gently for 4–5 minutes or
until the onion is soft but not coloured.

2 Meanwhile, rinse and dry the
chicken livers. Dry the calf's or
other liver, and slice into strips. Add the
liver to the pan and fry gently for a few
minutes until the strips are well sealed
on all sides.

3 Add half the wine and cook until
mostly evaporated, then add the
rest of the wine, tomato purée (paste),
half the parsley, anchovy fillets, stock or
water, a little salt and plenty of black
pepper.

4 Cover the pan and simmer for
15–20 minutes or until tender and
most of the liquid has been absorbed.

5 Cool the mixture a little then either
coarsely mince (grind) or put into a
food processor and process until coarsely
blended.

6 Return to the pan and add the
butter, remaining parsley and
capers and heat through gently until the
butter melts. Adjust the seasoning and
turn into a bowl. Serve warm or cold
spread on the slices of crusty bread and
sprinkled with chopped parsley.

CROSTINI

To make crostini, slice a crusty loaf or a
French loaf into small rounds or squares.
Heat olive oil in a frying pan (skillet) and
fry the slices until golden brown and crisp.
Drain on paper towels.

SEAFOOD SALAD

Fresh seafood is plentiful in Italy and varieties of seafood salads are found all over the regions. Each has its own speciality, depending on availability and what appears in each day's catch.

STEP 1

SERVES 4

175 g/6 oz squid rings, defrosted if frozen
600 ml/1 pint/2½ cups water
150 ml/¼ pint/⅔ cup dry white wine
250 g/8 oz hake or monkfish, cut into cubes
16–20 fresh mussels, scrubbed and beards
    removed
20 clams in shells, scrubbed, if available
    (otherwise use extra mussels)
125–175 g/4–6 oz peeled prawns (shrimp)
3–4 spring onions (scallions), trimmed and
    sliced (optional)
radicchio and endive (chicory) leaves, to
    serve
lemon wedges, to garnish

DRESSING:
6 tbsp olive oil
1 tbsp wine vinegar
2 tbsp chopped fresh parsley
1–2 garlic cloves, crushed
salt and pepper

GARLIC MAYONNAISE:
5 tbsp thick mayonnaise
2–3 tbsp fromage frais or natural yogurt
2 garlic cloves, crushed
1 tbsp capers
2 tbsp freshly chopped fresh parsley or
    mixed herbs

1 Poach the squid in the water and wine for 20 minutes or until nearly tender. Add the fish cubes and continue to cook gently for 7–8 minutes or until tender. Strain, reserving the fish, and place the stock in a clean pan.

2 Bring the fish stock to the boil and add the mussels and clams. Cover the pan and simmer gently for about 5 minutes or until the shells open. Discard any that stay closed.

3 Drain the shellfish and remove from their shells. Put into a bowl with the cooked fish and add the prawns (shrimp) and onions (scallions) if using.

4 For the dressing, whisk together the oil, vinegar, parsley, garlic, salt and plenty of black pepper. Pour over the fish, mix well, cover and chill for several hours. Combine all the ingredients for the garlic mayonnaise and chill.

5 Arrange small leaves of radicchio and endive (chicory) on 4 plates and spoon the fish salad into the centre. Garnish each plate with lemon wedges. Serve the garlic mayonnaise with the seafood salad.

STEP 2

STEP 3

STEP 4

CHAPTER TWO

Pasta & Pizza

It is well known that Italians are prolific eaters of pasta, but not everyone realizes just how many varieties of pasta are available; in fact there are many hundreds, and it would be almost impossible to list them all. Home-made pasta only takes a few minutes to cook while the bought variety takes longer, and it is best to follow the cooking directions on the pack. If you are going to make a lot of pasta it is worth investing in a pasta-making machine. Pasta is of Genoese origin but nowadays is even more popular in Naples and the southern regions of Italy, while in the north a fair amount of rice is consumed. Milanese and other risottos are made with short-grain Italian rice, the best of which is Arborio, but remember that this type of rice should never be rinsed before cooking. An Italian risotto is far moister than a pilau or other savoury rice, but it should not be soggy or sticky.

Gnocchi are made from cornmeal, potatoes or semolina, often combined with spinach and some sort of cheese. They resemble dumplings, and are either poached or baked, and served with some variety of cheese sauce. Polenta is made with either cornmeal or polenta flour and can be served either as a soft porridge or hard cake which is then fried. The traditional method of making polenta involved long, slow cooking, but now there is an excellent polenta mix available which cuts the time to 5 minutes!

Opposite: The market in the Piazza della Fratta, Padua, offers a wide selection of fruit and vegetables. Italians like to shop daily, to make sure their produce is absolutely fresh.

STEP 2

STEP 3

STEP 3

STEP 4

TORTELLINI

According to legend the shape of the tortellini is said to resemble the tummy button of Venus. Suffice to say that from this description, when you make tortellini you know exactly what they should look like!

SERVES 4

FILLING:
125 g/4 oz boneless, skinned chicken breast
60 g/2 oz Parma ham (prosciutto)
45 g/1½ oz cooked spinach, well drained
1 tbsp finely chopped onion
2 tbsp grated Parmesan cheese
good pinch ground allspice
1 egg, beaten
salt and pepper
1 quantity Pasta Dough (see pages 230–1)

SAUCE:
300 ml/½ pint/1¼ cups single (light)
 cream
1–2 garlic cloves, crushed
125 g/4 oz button mushrooms, sliced thinly
4 tbsp grated Parmesan cheese
1–2 tbsp chopped fresh flat-leaf parsley

1 Poach the chicken in well-seasoned water until tender, about 10 minutes; drain and chop roughly. When cool put into a food processor with the ham, spinach and onion and process until finely chopped, then add the Parmesan, allspice, egg and seasoning.

2 Roll out the pasta dough, half at a time, on a lightly floured work surface (counter) until thin.

3 Cut the dough into 4–5 cm/1½–2 inch rounds using a plain cutter. Place ½ teaspoon of the filling in the centre of each dough circle, fold the pieces in half to make a semi-circle and press the edges firmly together. Wrap around your index finger and cross over the 2 ends, pressing firmly together, curling the rest of the dough backwards to make a 'tummy button' shape. Slip the tortellini off your finger and lay on a lightly floured tray. Repeat with the rest of the dough, rerolling the trimmings.

4 Cook the tortellini in batches: heat a large pan of salted boiling water and add some tortellini. Bring back to the boil and once they rise to the surface cook for about 5 minutes, stirring occasionally. Remove with a perforated spoon, drain on paper towels and keep warm in a serving dish while cooking the remainder.

5 To make the sauce, heat the cream with the garlic in a pan and bring to the boil; simmer for a few minutes. Add the mushrooms and half the Parmesan, season, and simmer for 2–3 minutes. Stir in the parsley and pour over the warm tortellini. Sprinkle the tortellini with the remaining Parmesan and serve.

SICILIAN SPAGHETTI

*This delicious Sicilian dish originated as a handy way of using up
leftover cooked pasta. Any variety of long pasta could be used.*

STEP 1

SERVES 4
OVEN: 200°C/400°F/GAS MARK 6

2 aubergines (eggplants), about 650 g/1¼ lb
150 ml/¼ pint/⅔ cup olive oil
350 g/12 oz lean beef, finely minced
  (ground)
1 onion, chopped
2 garlic cloves, crushed
2 tbsp tomato purée (paste)
425 g/15 oz can peeled tomatoes, chopped
1 tsp Worcestershire sauce
1 tsp freshly chopped oregano or marjoram
  or ½ tsp dried oregano or marjoram
45 g/1½ oz pitted black olives, sliced
1 green, red or yellow (bell) pepper, cored,
  deseeded and chopped
175 g/6 oz spaghetti
125 g/4 oz/1 cup Parmesan cheese, grated
salt and pepper
oregano or parsley, to garnish (optional)

1 Brush a 20 cm/8 inch spring-release round cake tin (pan) with olive oil, place a disc of baking parchment in the base and oil. Trim the aubergines (eggplants) and cut into slanting slices about 5 mm/¼ inch thick. Heat some of the oil in a frying pan (skillet). Fry a few slices at a time in hot oil until lightly browned, turning once, and adding more oil as necessary. Drain on paper towels.

2 Put the minced (ground) beef, onion and garlic into a saucepan and cook, stirring frequently, until browned all over. Add the tomato purée (paste), tomatoes, Worcestershire sauce, herbs and seasoning and simmer for 10 minutes, stirring occasionally, then add the olives and (bell) pepper and continue for a further 10 minutes.

STEP 3

3 Heat a large pan of salted water and cook the spaghetti for 12–14 minutes until tender. Drain thoroughly. Turn the spaghetti into a bowl and mix in the meat mixture and Parmesan, combining thoroughly using 2 forks.

4 Lay overlapping slices of aubergine (eggplant) evenly over the base of the cake tin (pan) and up the sides. Add the meat mixture, pressing it down, and cover with the remaining slices of aubergine (eggplant).

STEP 4

5 Stand in a baking tin (pan) and cook in a preheated oven for 40 minutes. Leave to stand for 5 minutes. Loosen around the edges and invert on to a warmed serving dish, releasing the tin's (pan's) clip. Remove the parchment. Sprinkle with herbs before serving, if liked. Extra Parmesan may be offered.

STEP 4

GNOCCHI ROMANA

This is a traditional recipe from Piedmont. For a less rich version, omit the eggs. This is often served before a light main course, but it also makes an excellent main meal with a crisp salad.

STEP 1

SERVES 4
OVEN: 200°C/400°F/GAS MARK 6

750 ml/1¼ pints/ 3 cups milk
¼ tsp grated nutmeg
90 g/ 3 oz/6 tbsp butter, plus extra for greasing
250 g/8 oz/1⅓ cups semolina
125 g/4 oz/1 cup Parmesan cheese, grated finely
2 eggs, beaten
60 g/2 oz/½ cup Gruyère cheese, grated
salt and pepper
basil sprigs, to garnish

1 Bring the milk to the boil, remove from the heat and stir in the nutmeg, 30 g/1 oz/2 tablespoons butter and the seasonings. Whisk in the semolina gradually to prevent lumps forming and return to a low heat. Simmer gently for about 10 minutes, stirring constantly, until very thick.

2 Beat 60 g/2 oz/½ cup Parmesan into the semolina, followed by the eggs. Continue beating until the mixture is quite smooth.

3 Spread out the semolina mixture in an even layer on a sheet of baking parchment or in a large oiled baking

sheet (cookie sheet), smoothing the surface with a wet palette knife (spatula) – it should be about 1 cm/½ inch thick. Leave until cold, then chill for about 1 hour until firm.

4 Cut the gnocchi into circles of about 4 cm/1½ inch, using a plain greased biscuit (cookie) cutter.

5 Thoroughly grease a shallow ovenproof dish, or 4 individual dishes. Lay the gnocchi trimmings in the base of the dish and cover with overlapping circles of gnocchi. Melt the remaining butter and drizzle all over the gnocchi, then sprinkle first with the remaining Parmesan and then with the grated Gruyère.

6 Cook in a preheated oven for 25–30 minutes until the top is crisp and golden brown.

STEP 2

NOTE

Tomato and Pepper Sauce (see page 23) may be served with this dish, if liked.

STEP 3

35

STEP 4

POLENTA

Polenta is prepared and served in a variety of ways and can be enjoyed hot or cold, sweet or savoury. This is the traditional way of making it in Lombardy, although there is now an instant polenta mix available.

STEP 1

SERVES 4

1.5 litres/ 2¹/₃ pints/ 7 cups water
1¹/₂ tsp salt
300 g/ 10 oz/ 2 cups polenta or cornmeal
  flour
vegetable oil for frying and oiling
2 eggs, beaten (optional)
125 g/ 4 oz/ 2 cups fresh fine white
  breadcrumbs (optional)

MUSHROOM SAUCE:
3 tbsp olive oil
250 g/ 8 oz mushrooms, sliced
2 garlic cloves, crushed
150 ml/¹/₄ pint/²/₃ cup dry white wine
4 tbsp double (heavy) cream
2 tbsp chopped mixed fresh herbs
salt and pepper

STEP 2

1 Bring the water and salt to the boil in a large pan and gradually sprinkle in the polenta or cornmeal flour, stirring constantly to make sure the mixture is smooth, without lumps.

2 Simmer the mixture very gently, stirring frequently, until the polenta becomes very thick, 30–35 minutes. It is likely to splatter, in which case partially cover the pan with a lid. The mixture should become thick

STEP 3

enough for a wooden spoon to almost stand upright in it on its own.

3 Thoroughly oil a shallow tin (pan), about 28×18 cm/11×7 inches, and spoon in the polenta. Spread out evenly, using a wet palette knife (spatula), if necessary. Leave until cold then leave for a few hours at room temperature, if possible.

4 Cut the polenta into 30–36 squares. Heat the oil in a frying pan (skillet) and fry for about 5 minutes until the pieces are golden brown all over, turning them several times. Alternatively, dip each piece of polenta in beaten egg and coat in breadcrumbs before frying in the hot oil.

5 To make the mushroom sauce: heat the oil in a pan and fry the mushrooms with the crushed garlic for 3–4 minutes. Add the wine, season well and simmer for 5 minutes. Add the cream and chopped herbs and simmer for another minute or so.

6 Serve the polenta with the mushroom sauce. It could also be served with a tomato sauce, if preferred.

STEP 4

TAGLIATELLE WITH PUMPKIN

This unusual pasta dish comes from Emilia-Romagna.

STEP 1

STEP 2

STEP 3

STEP 3

SERVES 4

500 g/1 lb pumpkin or butternut squash
2 tbsp olive oil
1 onion, chopped finely
2 garlic cloves, crushed
4–6 tbsp freshly chopped parsley
good pinch ground or grated nutmeg
about 250 ml/8 fl oz/1 cup chicken or
   vegetable stock
125 g/4 oz Parma ham (prosciutto), cut
   into narrow strips
275 g/9 oz green or white tagliatelle, fresh
   or dried
150 ml/¼ pint/⅔ cup double (heavy)
   cream
salt and pepper
freshly grated Parmesan, to serve

1 Peel the pumpkin or butternut
squash, removing the hard layer
directly under the skin, and scoop out the
seeds and the membrane around them.
Cut the flesh into 1 cm/½ inch dice.

2 Heat the oil in a pan and fry the
onion and garlic gently until soft.
Add half the parsley and continue for a
minute or so longer.

3 Add the pumpkin or squash and
continue to cook for 2–3 minutes,

then season well with salt, pepper and
nutmeg and add half the stock. Bring to
the boil, cover and simmer for about 10
minutes or until the pumpkin is tender,
adding more stock as necessary. Add the
Parma ham (prosciutto) and continue to
cook for 2 minutes, stirring frequently.

4 Meanwhile, cook the tagliatelle in a
large saucepan of boiling salted
water, allowing 3–4 minutes for fresh
pasta or about 12 minutes for dried (or
follow the directions on the packet).
When *al dente*, drain thoroughly and
turn into a warmed serving bowl.

5 Add the cream to the ham mixture
and heat gently until really hot.
Adjust the seasoning and spoon over the
pasta. Sprinkle with the remaining
parsley and hand grated Parmesan
cheese separately.

FRESH PASTA

If you want to make your own pasta, use
the recipe for pasta dough (see pages
230–1), roll it out as thinly as possible and
cut into narrow strips. Allow to dry on a
cloth over a rack before cooking.

STEP 1

STEP 2

STEP 4

STEP 5

MILANESE RISOTTO

Italian rice is a round, short-grained variety with a nutty flavour, which is essential for a good risotto. Arborio is the very best kind to use.

SERVES 4–5

2 good pinches saffron threads
1 large onion, chopped finely
1–2 garlic cloves, crushed
90 g/3 oz/6 tbsp butter
350 g/12 oz/1²/₃ cups Arborio or other
    short-grain Italian rice
150 ml/¹/₄ pint/²/₃ cup dry white wine
1.25 litres/2 pints/5 cups boiling beef,
    chicken or vegetable stock,
90 g/3 oz/³/₄ cup Parmesan cheese, grated
salt and pepper

1 Put the saffron in a small bowl, cover with 3–4 tablespoons boiling water and leave to soak while cooking the risotto.

2 Fry the onion and garlic in 60 g/ 2 oz/4 tablespoons of the butter until soft but not coloured. Add the rice and continue to cook for a few minutes until all the grains are coated in butter and beginning to colour lightly.

3 Add the wine to the rice and simmer gently, stirring from time to time until it is all absorbed.

4 Add the boiling stock a little at a time, about 150 ml/¹/₄ pint/²/₃ cup,

cooking until the liquid is fully absorbed before adding more, and stirring frequently.

5 When all the stock is absorbed the rice should be tender but not soft and soggy. Stir in the saffron liquid, Parmesan, remaining butter and plenty of seasoning and simmer for a minute or so until piping hot and thoroughly mixed together.

6 Cover the pan tightly and leave to stand for 5 minutes off the heat. Give a good stir and serve at once.

COOKING RISOTTO

The finished dish should have moist but separate grains. This is achieved by adding the hot stock a little at a time, only adding more when the last addition is fully absorbed. Don't leave the risotto to cook by itself: it needs constant watching to see when more liquid is required.

STEP 1

STEP 2

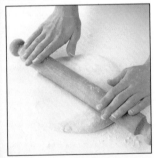

STEP 3

STEP 3

CALABRIAN PIZZA

Traditionally, a Calabrian pizza has a double layer of dough to make it robust and filling, but it can also be made as a single-layer pizza as shown here. Just double the amount of filling to make two single-layer pizzas.

SERVES 4–6
OVEN: 180°C/350°F/GAS MARK 4

400 g/14 oz/3½ cups plain (all-purpose) flour
½ tsp salt
1 sachet easy-blend yeast
2 tbsp olive oil
about 275 ml/9 fl oz/1 cup plus 2 tbsp warm water

FILLING:
2 tbsp olive oil
2 garlic cloves, crushed
1 red (bell) pepper, cored, deseeded and sliced
1 yellow (bell) pepper, cored, deseeded and sliced
125 g/4 oz Ricotta cheese
175 g/6 oz sun-dried tomatoes in oil, drained
3 hard-boiled (hard-cooked) eggs, sliced thinly
1 tbsp chopped mixed fresh herbs
125 g/4 oz salami, cut into strips
150–175 g/5–6 oz Mozzarella cheese, grated
a little milk, to glaze
salt and pepper

1 Sift the flour and salt into a bowl and mix in the yeast, then add the oil and enough warm water to mix to a smooth dough. Knead for 10–15 minutes by hand, or for 5 minutes with an electric mixer with a dough hook.

2 Shape the dough into a ball, place in a lightly oiled polythene bag and put in a warm place for 1–1½ hours or until doubled in size.

3 Heat the oil in a frying pan (skillet) and fry the garlic and (bell) peppers slowly in the oil until soft. Knock back (punch down) the dough and roll out half to fit the base of a 30 × 25 cm/12 × 10 inch oiled roasting tin (pan). Season and spread with the Ricotta, then cover with the tomatoes, eggs, herbs and pepper mixture. Arrange the salami strips on top and sprinkle with the grated cheese.

4 Roll out the remaining dough and place over the filling, pressing the edges together, or use to make a second pizza. Put to rise for about 1 hour in a warm place until puffed up. A single-layer pizza will take 30–40 minutes to rise.

5 Prick the double pizza with a fork about 20 times, brush the top with milk and bake for 50 minutes or until browned and firm. The single-layer pizza will take only 35–40 minutes. Serve hot.

CHAPTER THREE

Fish & Shellfish

Italians eat everything that comes out of the sea, from the smallest whitebait to the massive tuna fish, not forgetting the wide variety of shellfish. Fish markets in Italy are fascinating, with a huge variety of fish on display, but as most of the fish comes from the Mediterranean it is not always easy to find an equivalent elsewhere. However, imported frozen fish of all kinds is now appearing in fishmongers and supermarkets.

After pasta, fish is probably the most important source of food in Italy, and in many recipes fish or shellfish is combined with one type of pasta or another. The inland regions of Italy such as Lombardy and Umbria have lakes with plentiful supplies of fish, while Apulia has abundant supplies caught by offshore trawlers. The South has splendid fish, with tuna and swordfish taking pride of place, although red mullet and sea bass are plentiful and popular, too. Venice and surrounding areas have a wealth of fish and shellfish recipes, often combined with pasta, while the Ligurian coast is popular for fish soups and stews. The islands of Sicily and Sardinia abound with fish, which feature widely in their cuisine, from the large tuna to the sardines that give Sardinia its name.

Opposite: *The fishing fleet prepares to set off in the early morning light. Later in the day the catch – anything from John Dorey, bass, mullet, snapper and squid to lobsters and crabs – will be proudly displayed on the quayside, ready for the seafood market.*

STEP 2

STEP 2

STEP 4

STEP 4

BAKED SEA BASS

Sea bass is a delicious white-fleshed fish with a wonderful fresh flavour. If cooking two small fish, they can be grilled (broiled); if cooking one large fish, bake it in the oven.

SERVES 4
OVEN: 190°C/375°F/GAS MARK 5

1.4 kg/ 3 lb sea bass or 2 × 750 g/ 1¹/₂ lb
  sea bass, gutted
2–4 sprigs fresh rosemary
¹/₂ lemon, sliced thinly
2 tbsp olive oil
bay leaves and lemon wedges, to garnish

GARLIC SAUCE:
2 tsp coarse sea salt
2 tsp capers
2 garlic cloves, crushed
4 tbsp water
2 fresh bay leaves
1 tsp lemon juice or wine vinegar
2 tbsp olive oil
black pepper

1 Scrape off the scales from the fish and cut off the sharp fins. Make diagonal cuts along both sides. Wash and dry thoroughly.

2 Place a sprig of rosemary in the cavity of each of the smaller fish with half the lemon slices; or 2 sprigs and all the lemon in the large fish. To grill (broil), place in a foil-lined pan, brush lightly with 1–2 tablespoons oil and grill (broil) under a medium heat for about 5 minutes on each side or until cooked through, turning carefully.

3 To bake: place the fish in a foil-lined dish or roasting tin (pan) brushed with oil, and brush the fish with the rest of the oil. Bake in a preheated oven for about 30 minutes for the small fish or 45–50 minutes for the large fish, until tender when tested with a skewer.

4 To make the sauce: crush the salt and capers with the garlic in a pestle and mortar if available and then gradually work in the water. Alternatively, put it all into a food processor or blender and switch on until smooth. Bruise the bay leaves and remaining sprigs of rosemary and put in a bowl. Add the garlic mixture, lemon juice or vinegar and oil and pound together until the flavours are released. Season with black pepper.

5 Place the fish on a serving dish and, if liked, carefully remove the skin. Spoon some of the sauce over the fish and serve the rest separately. Garnish with fresh bay leaves and lemon wedges.

STEP 2

STEP 4

STEP 5

STEP 5

SARDINE & POTATO BAKE

Fresh sardines bear very little resemblance to the canned varieties. They are readily available, frozen and sometimes fresh, so this traditional dish from Liguria can now be enjoyed by all.

SERVES 4
OVEN: 190°C/375°F/GAS MARK 5

1 kg/2 lb potatoes, peeled
1 kg/2 lb sardines, defrosted if frozen
1 tbsp olive oil, plus extra for oiling
1 onion, chopped
2–3 garlic cloves, crushed
2 tbsp chopped fresh flat-leaf parsley
350 g/12 oz ripe tomatoes, peeled and sliced
  or 425 g/15 oz can peeled tomatoes,
  partly drained and chopped
1–2 tbsp chopped fresh Italian herbs (e.g.
  oregano, thyme, rosemary, marjoram)
150 ml/¼ pint/⅔ cup dry white wine
salt and pepper

1 Put the potatoes in a pan of salted water, bring to the boil, cover and simmer for 10 minutes, then drain. When cool enough to handle, cut into slices about 5 mm/¼ inch thick.

2 Gut and clean the sardines: cut off their heads and tails and then slit open the length of the belly. Turn the fish over so the skin is upwards and press firmly along the backbone to loosen the bones. Turn over again and carefully remove the backbone. Wash the fish in cold water, drain well and dry them on paper towels.

3 Heat the oil in a pan and fry the onion and garlic until soft, but not coloured.

4 Arrange the potatoes in a well-oiled ovenproof dish and sprinkle with the onion and garlic and then the parsley and plenty of seasoning.

5 Lay the open sardines over the potatoes, skin-side down, then cover with the tomatoes and the rest of the herbs. Pour on the wine and season again.

6 Cook uncovered in a preheated oven for about 40 minutes until the fish is tender. If the casserole seems to be drying out, add another 2 tablespoons of wine.

VARIATION

Fresh anchovies may be used in this recipe in place of sardines. Prepare in the same way.

STEP 1

STEP 3

STEP 4

STEP 5

TROUT IN RED WINE

This recipe from Trentino is best when the fish are freshly caught, but it is a good way to cook any trout, giving it an interesting flavour.

SERVES 4

4 fresh trout, about 300 g/10 oz each
250 ml/8 fl oz/1 cup red or white wine
   vinegar
300 ml/¹/₂ pint/1¹/₄ cups red or dry white
   wine
150 ml/¹/₄ pint/²/₃ cup water
1 carrot, sliced
2–4 bay leaves
thinly pared rind of 1 lemon
1 small onion, sliced very thinly
4 sprigs fresh parsley
4 sprigs fresh thyme
1 tsp black peppercorns
6–8 whole cloves
90 g/3 oz/6 tbsp butter
1 tbsp chopped fresh mixed herbs
   or parsley
salt and pepper
fresh herbs and lemon slices, to garnish

1 Gut the trout but leave their heads on. Dry on paper towels and lay the fish head to tail in a shallow container or baking tin (pan) just large enough to hold them in a single layer.

2 Bring the wine vinegar to the boil and pour slowly all over the fish. Leave the fish to marinate for about 20 minutes.

3 Put the wine, water, carrot, bay leaves, lemon rind, onion, herbs, peppercorns and cloves into a pan with a good pinch of sea salt and heat gently.

4 Drain the fish thoroughly, discarding the vinegar. Place the fish in a fish kettle or large frying pan (skillet) so they touch. When the wine mixture boils, strain gently over the fish so they are about half covered. Cover the pan and simmer very gently over a low heat for 15 minutes.

5 Carefully remove the fish from the liquid, draining off as much as possible, and arrange on a serving dish.

6 Boil the cooking liquid hard until it is reduced to 4–6 tablespoons. Melt the butter in a small saucepan and strain in the cooking liquid. Adjust the seasoning and spoon the sauce over the fish. Sprinkle with chopped mixed herbs and garnish with lemon and sprigs of fresh herbs.

SQUID CASSEROLE

Squid and octopus are great favourites in Italy and around the Mediterranean resorts. Squid is often served fried, but here it is casseroled with tomatoes and (bell) peppers to give a rich sauce.

STEP 1

STEP 1

STEP 2

STEP 3

SERVES 4
OVEN: 180°C/350°F/GAS MARK 4

1 kg/2 lb whole squid or 750 g/1½ lb squid
   rings, defrosted if frozen
3 tbsp olive oil
1 large onion, sliced thinly
2 garlic cloves, crushed
1 red (bell) pepper, cored, deseeded and sliced
1–2 sprigs fresh rosemary
150 ml/¼ pint/⅔ cup dry white wine and
   250 ml/8 fl oz/1 cup water, or 350 ml/
   12 fl oz/1½ cups water or fish stock
425 g/15 oz can peeled tomatoes, chopped
2 tbsp tomato purée (paste)
1 tsp paprika
salt and pepper
fresh rosemary or parsley sprigs, to garnish
   (optional)

1 Prepare the squid (see below right) and cut into 1 cm/½ inch slices; cut the tentacles into lengths of about 5 cm/ 2 inches. If using frozen squid rings, make sure they are fully defrosted and well drained.

2 Heat the oil in a flameproof casserole and fry the onion and garlic gently until soft. Add the squid rings, increase the heat and continue to cook for about 10 minutes until sealed

and beginning to colour lightly. Add the red (bell) pepper, rosemary and wine (if using), and water or stock and bring up to the boil. Cover and simmer gently for 45 minutes.

3 Discard the rosemary sprigs (but don't take out any leaves that have come off). Add the tomatoes, tomato purée (paste), seasoning and paprika. Continue to simmer gently for 45–60 minutes, or cover the casserole tightly and cook in a preheated oven for 45–60 minutes until tender.

4 Give the sauce a good stir and adjust the seasoning. Garnish with rosemary or parsley, if liked, and serve with lots of crusty bread.

TO PREPARE SQUID

Peel off as much as possible of the fine outer skin, using your fingers, then cut off the head and tentacles. Extract the transparent flat oval bone from the body and discard. Carefully remove the sac of black ink, then turn the body sac inside out. Wash thoroughly in cold water. Cut off the tentacles from the head and discard the rest; wash thoroughly.

CHAPTER FOUR

Meat & Poultry

Italians tend to have their own special way of butchering meat, producing very different cuts. Most of their meat is sold boned and often cut straight across the grain. They tend to serve prime cuts and steaks very rare, so great care needs to be taken when ordering in a restaurant. Veal is a great favourite in Italy and widely available, with the popular cuts for escalopes always made straight across the grain of the meat. It is then beaten out thinly, using a meat mallet. Pork is also popular, with roast pig the traditional dish of Umbria. Suckling pig is roasted with lots of fresh herbs, especially rosemary, until the skin is crisp and brown. Lamb is often served for special occasions, cooked on a spit or roasted in the oven with wine, garlic and herbs; and the very small cutlets from young lambs feature widely, especially in Rome. Offal plays an important role in Italian cooking with liver, brains, sweetbreads, tongue, heart, tripe and kidneys, from both veal and lamb, always available.

Poultry dishes provide some of Italy's finest food. Every part of the chicken is used, including the feet and innards for making soup. It is the spit-roasted chicken, flavoured strongly with rosemary, that has become almost a national Italian dish, being sold all over the country. Turkey, duck, goose and guinea fowl are also popular, as is game. Wild rabbit and hare, wild boar and deer are also available, especially in Sardinia.

Opposite: *Italians take their food very seriously, so eating out is a very popular activity. Blessed with a wonderful climate, they can often eat outdoors, as in this Venetian restaurant.*

PIZZAIOLA STEAK

This has a Neapolitan sauce, using the delicious red tomatoes so abundant in that area, but canned ones make an excellent alternative.

SERVES 4

*2 × 425 g / 15 oz cans peeled tomatoes or
   750 g / 1 ½ lb fresh tomatoes*
4 tbsp olive oil
2–3 garlic cloves, crushed
1 onion, chopped finely
1 tbsp tomato purée (paste)
*1 ½ tsp freshly chopped marjoram or
   oregano or ¾ tsp dried marjoram or
   oregano*
4 thin sirloin or rump steaks
2 tbsp chopped fresh flat-leaf parsley
1 tsp sugar
salt and pepper
fresh herbs, to garnish (optional)
sauté potatoes, to serve

1 If using canned tomatoes, purée them in a food processor, then sieve (strain) to remove the seeds. If using fresh tomatoes, peel, remove the seeds and chop finely.

2 Heat half the oil in a pan and fry the garlic and onions very gently for about 5 minutes until soft.

3 Add the tomatoes, seasoning, tomato purée (paste) and chopped herbs to the pan. If using fresh tomatoes add 4 tablespoons water too, and then

STEP 3

simmer very gently for 8–10 minutes, giving an occasional stir.

4 Meanwhile, trim the steaks if necessary and season with salt and pepper. Heat the remaining oil in a frying pan (skillet) and fry the steaks quickly on both sides to seal, then continue until cooked to your liking – 2 minutes for rare, 3–4 minutes for medium, or 5 minutes for well done. Alternatively, cook the steaks under a hot grill (broiler) after brushing lightly with oil.

STEP 4

5 When the sauce has thickened a little, adjust the seasoning and stir in the chopped parsley and sugar to taste.

6 Pour off the excess fat from the pan with the steaks and add the tomato sauce. Reheat gently and serve at once, with the sauce spooned over and around the steaks. Garnish with fresh herbs, if liked. Sauté potatoes make a good accompaniment with a green vegetable.

STEP 5

ALTERNATIVE

This sauce can be served with veal and chicken. It can also be served with grilled (broiled) or baked white fish.

STEP 6

STEP 1

STEP 2

STEP 3

STEP 4

VITELLO TONNATO

Veal dishes are the speciality of Lombardy, with this dish being one of the more sophisticated. Serve cold, either as part of an antipasto or as a main course. It is best served with seasonal salads.

SERVES 4

750 g/ 1½ lb boned leg of veal, rolled
2 bay leaves
10 black peppercorns
2–3 whole cloves
½ tsp salt
2 carrots, sliced
1 onion, sliced
2 celery sticks, sliced
about 750 ml/ 1¼ pints / 3 cups stock or
    water
150 ml/¼ pint/⅔ cup dry white wine
    (optional)

TUNA SAUCE:
90 g/ 3 oz canned tuna fish, well drained
50 g (1½ oz) can anchovy fillets, drained
150 ml/¼ pint/⅔ cup olive oil
2 tsp capers
2 egg yolks
1 tbsp lemon juice
salt and pepper

TO GARNISH:
capers
lemon wedges
fresh herbs

1 Put the veal in a saucepan with the bay leaves, peppercorns, cloves, salt and vegetables. Add sufficient stock or water and the wine (if using) to barely cover the veal. Bring to the boil, remove any scum, then cover the pan and simmer gently for 1 hour or until tender. Leave in the water until cold, then drain thoroughly. If time allows, chill the veal once it is cool to make it easier to carve.

2 To make the tuna sauce: mash the tuna fish with 4 anchovy fillets and 1 tablespoon oil and the capers, then add the egg yolks and press the mixture through a sieve (strainer) or purée in a food processor or blender until smooth.

3 Stir in the lemon juice then gradually whisk in the rest of the oil a few drops at a time until the sauce is smooth and has the consistency of thick cream. Season to taste.

4 Slice the veal thinly and arrange on a flat platter in overlapping slices. Spoon the tuna fish sauce over the veal to cover. Then cover the dish and chill overnight.

5 Before serving, uncover the veal and arrange the remaining anchovy fillets and the capers in a decorative pattern on top. Garnish with lemon wedges and herbs.

STEP 1

STEP 3

STEP 4

STEP 6

POT ROAST LEG OF LAMB

This dish from the Abruzzi is even better if you use a leg of mutton in place of lamb: the meat absorbs the flavours even better and becomes very tender, giving a truly memorable dish.

SERVES 4
OVEN: 180°C/350°F/GAS MARK 4

1.75 kg/ 3½ lb leg of lamb
3–4 sprigs fresh rosemary
125 g/4 oz streaky bacon slices
4 tbsp olive oil
2–3 garlic cloves, crushed
2 onions, sliced
2 carrots, sliced
2 celery sticks, sliced
300 ml/½ pint/ 1¼ cups dry white wine
1 tbsp tomato purée (paste)
300 ml/½ pint/ 1¼ cups stock
350 g/ 12 oz tomatoes, peeled, quartered
    and seeded
1 tbsp chopped flat-leaf fresh parsley
1 tbsp chopped fresh oregano or marjoram
salt and pepper
fresh rosemary sprigs, to garnish

1 Wipe the joint of lamb all over, trim off any excess fat, then season the joint well with salt and pepper, rubbing well in. Lay the fresh rosemary sprigs over the lamb, cover evenly with the bacon slices and tie in place with fine kitchen string.

2 Heat the oil in a frying pan (skillet) and fry the lamb for about 10 minutes until browned all over, turning it over several times. Remove the lamb from the pan.

3 Transfer the oil from the pan to a large flameproof casserole and fry the garlic and onions together for 3–4 minutes until beginning to soften. Add the carrots and celery and continue to cook for a few minutes longer, stirring occasionally.

4 Lay the lamb on top of the vegetables and press well to partly bury. Pour the wine over the lamb, add the tomato purée (paste) and simmer for 3–4 minutes. Add the stock, tomatoes and herbs and plenty of seasoning and bring back to the boil for a further 3–4 minutes.

5 Cover the casserole tightly and cook in a preheated oven for 2–2½ hours until very tender.

6 Remove the lamb from the casserole and if liked, take off the bacon and herbs along with the string. Keep warm. Strain the juices, skimming off any excess fat, and serve in a jug. The vegetables may be put around the joint or in a serving dish. Garnish with fresh rosemary sprigs.

STEP 2

STEP 3

STEP 4

STEP 5

SALTIMBOCCA

*Literally translated saltimbocca means 'jump in the mouth',
and this quick, tasty veal dish almost does that.*

SERVES 4

4 thin veal escalopes
8 fresh sage leaves
4 thin slices Parma ham (prosciutto), same
*   size as the veal*
flour for dredging
2 tbsp olive oil
30 g/1 oz/2 tbsp butter
4 tbsp white wine
4 tbsp chicken stock
4 tbsp Marsala
salt and pepper
fresh sage leaves, to garnish

1 Either leave the escalopes as they are or cut in half. Place the pieces of veal on a sheet of clingfilm (plastic wrap) or baking parchment, keeping them well apart, and cover with a second sheet.

2 Using a meat mallet or rolling pin, beat the escalopes gently until they are at least twice their original size and very thin.

3 Lightly season the veal escalopes with salt and pepper and lay 2 fresh sage leaves on the large slices, or one on each of the smaller slices. Then lay the Parma ham (prosciutto) slices evenly over the escalopes to cover the sage and fit the size of the veal.

4 Secure the ham to the veal with wooden cocktail sticks (toothpicks). If preferred, the large slices can be folded in half first. Dredge lightly with flour.

5 Heat the olive oil and butter in a large frying pan (skillet) and fry the escalopes until golden brown each side and just cooked through – about 4 minutes for single slices or 5–6 minutes for double ones. Take care not to overcook. Remove to a serving dish and keep warm.

6 Add the wine, stock and Marsala to the pan and bring to the boil, stirring to loosen all the sediment from the pan. Boil until reduced by almost half. Adjust the seasoning and quickly pour over the saltimbocca. Serve at once, garnished with fresh sage leaves.

ALTERNATIVE

This dish can also be made using boneless chicken breasts. Slit the breasts almost in half, open out and beat as thinly as possible, as for the veal.

CHICKEN WITH GREEN OLIVES

*Olives are a popular flavouring for poultry and game in Apulia, where
this recipe originates. In Italy every morsel of the bird is used
in some way, most often for soups and stock.*

STEP 1

SERVES 4
OVEN: 180°C/350°F/GAS MARK 4

4 chicken breasts, part boned
2 tbsp olive oil
30 g/1 oz/2 tbsp butter
1 large onion, chopped finely
2 garlic cloves, crushed
2 red, yellow or green (bell) peppers, cored,
  deseeded and cut into large pieces
250 g/8 oz large closed-cup mushrooms,
  sliced or quartered
175 g/6 oz tomatoes, peeled and halved
150 ml/¼ pint/⅔ cup dry white wine
125–175 g/4–6 oz green olives, pitted
4–6 tbsp double (heavy) cream
salt and pepper
chopped fresh flat-leaf parsley, to garnish

1 Season the chicken. Heat the oil
and butter in a frying pan (skillet).
Add the chicken and fry until browned
all over. Remove from the pan.

2 Add the onion and garlic to the
pan and fry gently until beginning
to soften. Add the (bell) peppers to the
pan with the mushrooms and continue
to cook for a few minutes longer.

3 Add the tomatoes and plenty of
seasoning to the pan and then

transfer the vegetable mixture to an
ovenproof casserole. Place the chicken
on the bed of vegetables.

4 Add the wine to the frying pan
(skillet) and bring to the boil. Pour
the wine over the chicken and cover the
casserole tightly. Cook in a preheated
oven for 50 minutes.

5 Add the olives to the chicken, mix
lightly then pour on the cream.
Re-cover the casserole and return to the
oven for 10–20 minutes or until the
chicken is very tender.

6 Adjust the seasoning and serve the
pieces of chicken, surrounded by
the vegetables and sauce, with pasta or
tiny new potatoes. Sprinkle with parsley
to garnish.

NOODLES

Serve this dish with freshly made
ribbon noodles for a really attractive
presentation. Fresh pasta takes only 2–3
minutes to cook.

STEP 2

STEP 3

STEP 5

LIVER WITH WINE SAUCE

Liver is popular in Italy and is served in many ways. The ideal is calf's liver, but this is expensive and not always readily available, so use lamb's liver as an alternative.

SERVES 4

4 slices calf's liver or 8 slices lamb's liver, about 500 g/1 lb
flour for coating
1 tbsp olive oil
30 g/1 oz/2 tbsp butter
125 g/4 oz lean bacon slices, rinded
1 onion, chopped
1 garlic clove, crushed
1 celery stick, sliced thinly
150 ml/¼ pint/⅔ cup red wine
150 ml/¼ pint/⅔ cup beef stock
good pinch ground allspice
1 tsp Worcestershire sauce
1 tsp freshly chopped sage or ½ tsp dried sage
3–4 tomatoes, peeled
salt and pepper
fresh sage leaves, to garnish

1 Wipe the liver, season with salt and pepper and coat lightly in flour, shaking off the surplus.

2 Heat the oil and butter in a pan and fry the liver until well sealed on both sides and just cooked through – take care not to overcook. Remove the liver from the pan, cover and keep warm.

3 Cut the bacon into narrow strips and add to the fat left in the pan with the onion, garlic and celery. Fry gently until soft.

4 Add the wine and stock, allspice, Worcestershire sauce, sage and salt and pepper. Bring to the boil and simmer for 3–4 minutes.

5 Quarter the tomatoes, discard the seeds and cut each piece in half. Add to the sauce and continue to cook for a couple of minutes.

6 Serve the liver on a little of the sauce, with the remainder spooned over. Garnish with fresh sage leaves and serve with boiled tiny new potatoes or sauté potatoes.

COOKING LIVER

Overcooked liver is dry and tasteless, especially when it is coated in flour. Cook the slices for only 2–3 minutes on each side – they should be soft and tender, and still a little pink in the centre.

CHAPTER FIVE

Desserts

Many Italians prefer to finish their meal with a bowl of mixed fruits or fruits with cheese, but they do like their desserts too. When there is a family gathering or a celebration, a special effort is made and the delicacies appear. The Sicilians are said to have the sweetest tooth of all, and many Italian desserts are thought to have originated there. Ice cream (*gelato*), sorbet and water ice (*granita*) are said to be borrowed from the Arabs, who occupied Sicily centuries ago, and you have to go a very long way to beat a Sicilian ice cream, especially the famous cassata and Ricotta ice creams.

Fruits feature in desserts too. The famous pear tarts of the north are mouthwatering, using the very best fruit blended with apricot jam, sultanas (golden raisins) and almonds, while oranges appear marinated in syrup and liqueur. Biscuits (cookies) with almond flavouring are often served as an accompaniment, and the famous florentines – biscuits (cookies) full of glacé (candied) fruit and covered with chocolate – are favourites. Gâteaux are also popular, often incorporating Mascarpone or Ricotta along with citrus fruits and honey. Tiramisu is a favourite with all, and for Christmas and special occasions try the honey cake from Siena called Panforte – so very rich that even a tiny piece will leave you with delicious memories for a very long time.

Opposite: *The fertile plains of Tuscany grow an enormous variety of fruit and vegetables. Many famous desserts originate here, including the luscious Panforte di Siena.*

TIRAMISU

A favourite Italian dessert which is found in many regions. Here it is flavoured with coffee and Amaretto, but you could also use Marsala and Maraschino.

STEP 1

STEP 1

STEP 4

STEP 5

SERVES 4–6

20–24 sponge fingers (lady-fingers), about
    150 g/5 oz
2 tbsp cold black coffee
2 tbsp coffee flavouring (extract)
2 tbsp Amaretto or brandy
4 egg yolks
90 g/3 oz/6 tbsp caster (superfine) sugar
few drops vanilla flavouring (extract)
grated rind of ½ lemon
350 g/12 oz/1½ cups Mascarpone cheese
2 tsp lemon juice
250 ml/8 fl oz/1 cup double (heavy) cream
1 tbsp milk
30 g/1 oz/¼ cup flaked (slivered) almonds,
    lightly toasted
2 tbsp cocoa powder
1 tbsp icing (confectioners') sugar

1 Arrange almost half the sponge fingers (lady-fingers) in the base of a glass bowl or serving dish. Combine the black coffee, coffee flavouring (extract) and Amaretto or brandy and sprinkle just over half the mixture over the fingers.

2 Put the egg yolks into a heatproof bowl with the sugar, vanilla flavouring (extract) and lemon rind. Stand over a saucepan of gently simmering water and whisk until very thick and creamy and the whisk leaves a very heavy trail when lifted from the bowl.

3 Put the Mascarpone into a bowl, add the lemon juice and beat until the mixture is smooth.

4 Combine the egg mixture and Mascarpone mixture until evenly blended, then pour half over the sponge fingers (lady-fingers) and spread out evenly.

5 Add another layer of sponge fingers (lady-fingers), sprinkle with the remaining coffee mixture and then cover with the remaining cheese mixture. Chill for at least 2 hours and preferably overnight.

6 To serve, whip the cream and milk together until fairly stiff and spread or pipe over the dessert. Sprinkle with the flaked (slivered) almonds and then sift an even layer of cocoa powder over so the top is completely covered. Finally sift a very light layer of icing (confectioners') sugar over the cocoa powder.

ZABAGLIONE

This light dessert is reminiscent of a whisked egg custard. Serve warm or chilled, accompanied by sponge fingers (lady-fingers) or amaretti biscuits (cookies), and soft fruits such as strawberries or raspberries.

STEP 1

SERVES 4

6 egg yolks
90 g / 3 oz / 6 tbsp caster (superfine) sugar
6 tbsp Marsala
amaretti biscuits (cookies) or sponge fingers
   (lady-fingers) (optional)
strawberries or raspberries (optional)

1 Put the egg yolks into a heatproof bowl and whisk until a pale yellow colour, using a rotary, balloon or electric whisk.

2 Whisk in the sugar, followed by the Marsala, continuing to whisk all the time.

3 Stand the bowl over a saucepan of very gently simmering water, or transfer to the top of a double boiler, and continue to whisk constantly, scraping around the sides of the bowl from time to time. Whisk until the mixture thickens sufficiently to stand in soft peaks. On no account allow the water to boil or the zabaglione will overcook and turn into scrambled eggs.

4 As soon as the mixture is thick and foamy, take it from the heat and whisk for a couple of minutes longer.

5 Pour immediately into stemmed glasses and serve warm, or leave until cold and serve chilled.

6 Fruits such as strawberries or raspberries or crumbled sponge fingers (lady-fingers) or amaretti biscuits (cookies) may be placed in the base of the glasses before adding the zabaglione.

STEP 2

STEP 3

STEP 4

VARIATION

Any other type of liqueur may be used in place of Marsala, for a change.

STEP 1

STEP 2

STEP 3

STEP 4

PANFORTE DI SIENA

This famous Tuscan honey and nut cake is a Christmas speciality. In Italy it is sold in pretty boxes, which seems to make it taste even better. Panforte is very rich and sticky and should be served in very thin slices.

SERVES 12
OVEN: 150°C/300°F/GAS MARK 2

125 g/4 oz/1 cup split whole almonds
125 g/4 oz/³/4 cup hazelnuts
90 g/3 oz/¹/2 cup cut mixed (candied) peel
60 g/2 oz/¹/2 cup no-need-to-soak dried apricots
60 g/2 oz glacé (candied) or crystallized pineapple
grated rind of 1 large orange
60 g/2 oz/¹/2 cup plain (all-purpose) flour
2 tbsp cocoa powder
2 tsp ground cinnamon
125 g/4 oz/¹/2 cup caster (superfine) sugar
175 g/6 oz/¹/2 cup honey
icing (confectioners') sugar for dredging

1 Toast the almonds until lightly browned and place in a bowl. Toast the hazelnuts under the grill (broiler) until the skins split. Place the hazelnuts on a towel and rub off the skins with the towel. Roughly chop the hazelnuts and add to the almonds with the mixed (candied) peel.

2 Chop the apricots and pineapple fairly finely, add to the nuts with the orange rind and mix well.

3 Sift the flour with the cocoa and cinnamon, add to the nut mixture and mix evenly.

4 Line a round 20 cm/8 inch cake tin (pan) or deep loose-based flan tin (pan) with baking parchment.

5 Put the sugar and honey into a saucepan and heat until the sugar dissolves, then boil gently for about 5 minutes or until the mixture thickens and begins to turn a deeper shade of brown. Quickly add to the nut mixture and stir through it evenly. Turn into the prepared tin (pan) and level the top with the help of a damp spoon.

6 Bake in a preheated oven for 1 hour. Remove from the oven and leave in the tin (pan) until cold. Take out of the tin (pan) and carefully peel off the parchement. Dredge the cake heavily with sifted icing (confectioners') sugar. Serve cut into very thin slices.

STORAGE

Panforte will keep for several weeks stored in an airtight container or securely wrapped in foil.

PEAR TART

Pears are a very popular fruit in Italy. In this recipe from Trentino they are flavoured with almonds, cinnamon, raisins and apricot jam, then baked in an open tart with a soft-textured sweet pastry case (shell).

STEP 1

SERVES 4–6
OVEN: 200°C/400°F/GAS MARK 6

275 g/9 oz/2¼ cups plain (all-purpose)
 flour
pinch salt
125 g/4 oz/½ cup caster (superfine) sugar
125 g/4 oz/½ cup butter, diced
1 egg
1 egg yolk
few drops vanilla flavouring (extract)
2–3 tsp water

FILLING:
4 tbsp apricot jam
60 g/2 oz amaretti or ratafia biscuits
 (cookies), crumbled
850–1 kg/1¾–2 lb pears, peeled and cored
1 tsp ground cinnamon
90 g/3 oz/½ cup raisins or sultanas (golden
 raisins)
60 g/2 oz/⅓ cup soft brown sugar
sifted icing (confectioners') sugar for
 sprinkling

1 Sift the flour and salt on to a flat surface, make a well in the centre and add the sugar, butter, egg, egg yolk, vanilla and most of the water.

2 Using your fingers, gradually work the flour into the other ingredients to give a smooth pliable dough, adding a little more water, if necessary. Wrap in clingfilm (plastic wrap) and chill for 1 hour or until firm. Alternatively, put all the ingredients into a food processor and process until evenly blended and smooth.

STEP 3

3 Roll out almost three-quarters of the dough and line a shallow 25cm/10 inch flan tin (pan). Spread the apricot jam over the base and sprinkle with the crushed biscuits (cookies).

4 Slice the pears very thinly. Arrange the pear slices over the biscuits (cookies) in the pastry (dough) case. Sprinkle first with cinnamon then with raisins, and finally with the brown sugar.

STEP 4

5 Roll out a thin rope shape using about one-third of the remaining dough, and place around the edge of the tart. Roll the remainder into thin ropes and arrange in a lattice over the top, 4 or 5 strips in each direction, attaching to the strip around the edge.

6 Bake in a preheated oven for about 50 minutes until golden. Remove from the oven and leave to cool. Serve warm or chilled, sprinkled with sifted icing (confectioners') sugar.

STEP 5

CARAMELIZED ORANGES

The secret of these oranges is to allow them to marinate in the syrup for at least 24 hours, and preferably longer, so the caramel and liqueur can penetrate to the centre of the fruit.

STEP 3

SERVES 6

6 large oranges
250 g / 8 oz / 1 heaped cup caster (superfine)
or granulated sugar
250 ml / 8 fl oz / 1 cup water
6 whole cloves (optional)
2–4 tbsp orange-flavour liqueur or brandy

1 Use a citrus zester or potato peeler to pare off the rind from 2 oranges, to give narrow strips of rind without any of the white pith attached. If using a potato peeler, cut the rind into very thin julienne strips using a very sharp knife.

2 Put the strips into a small saucepan and barely cover with water. Bring to the boil and simmer for 5 minutes until tender. Drain the strips well and reserve the water.

3 Cut away all the white pith and peel from the oranges using a very sharp knife and then cut each orange horizontally into 4 slices. Reassemble the oranges and hold in place with wooden cocktail sticks (toothpicks). Stand the oranges in a heatproof dish.

4 Put the sugar and water into a heavy-based saucepan with the

cloves, if using. Bring to the boil and simmer gently until the sugar has dissolved, then boil hard without stirring until the syrup thickens and begins to turn brown. Continue to cook until it is light golden brown, then quickly remove from the heat and carefully pour in the reserved liquid from cooking the rinds.

5 Return to a gentle heat until the caramel has fully dissolved again, then remove from the heat and add the liqueur or brandy. When mixed pour over the oranges.

6 Sprinkle the orange strips over the oranges, cover with clingfilm (plastic wrap) and leave until cold. Chill for at least 3 hours and preferably for 24–48 hours. Spoon the syrup over the oranges several times while they are marinating. Discard the cocktail sticks (toothpicks) before serving.

STEP 4

STEP 5

CARAMEL

To make caramel, sugar syrup is boiled until it turns golden brown and reaches the 'small crack' stage, a temperature of 138–152°C/280–305°F on a sugar (candy) thermometer.

STEP 6

STEP 1

STEP 2

STEP 4

STEP 5

RICOTTA ICE CREAM

Ice cream is one of the traditional dishes of Italy. Everyone eats it and there are numerous gelato stalls selling a wide variety of flavours, usually in a cone. It is also served sliced, as in this classic from Sicily.

SERVES 4–6

30 g/ 1 oz/ ¼ cup pistachio nuts
30 g/ 1 oz/ ¼ cup walnuts or pecan nuts
30 g/ 1 oz/ ¼ cup toasted chopped hazelnuts
grated rind of 1 orange
grated rind of 1 lemon
30 g/ 1 oz/ 2 tbsp stem (candied) ginger
30 g/ 1 oz/ 2 tbsp glacé (candied) cherries
30 g/ 1 oz/ ¼ cup no-need-to-soak dried apricots
30 g/ 1 oz/ 2 tbsp raisins
500 g/ 1 lb/ 1½ cups Ricotta cheese
2 tbsp Maraschino, Amaretto or brandy
1 tsp vanilla flavouring (extract)
4 egg yolks
125 g/ 4 oz/ ½ cup caster (superfine) sugar

TO DECORATE:
whipped cream
few glacé (candied) cherries, pistachio nuts or mint leaves

1 Roughly chop the pistachio nuts and walnuts and mix with the hazelnuts and orange and lemon rinds. Finely chop the ginger, cherries, apricots and raisins and add to the bowl.

2 Mix the Ricotta evenly through the fruit mixture, then beat in the liqueur and vanilla flavouring (extract).

3 Put the egg yolks and sugar in a bowl and whisk hard until very thick and creamy – they may be whisked over a pan of gently simmering water to speed up the process. Leave to cool, if necessary.

4 Carefully fold the Ricotta mixture evenly through the beaten eggs and sugar until smooth.

5 Line a 18 × 12 cm/ 7 × 5 inch loaf tin (pan) with a double layer of clingfilm (plastic wrap) or baking parchment. Pour in the Ricotta mixture, level the top, cover with more clingfilm (plastic wrap) or baking parchment and freeze until firm – at least overnight.

6 To serve, carefully remove the ice cream from the tin (pan) and peel off the lining. Stand on a serving dish and if liked, decorate with whipped cream using a piping bag and star nozzle (tip), and glacé (candied) cherries and/or pistachio nuts. Serve in slices, with mint leaves, if liked.

FIRST COURSES

•

PASTA WITH MEAT SAUCES

•

PASTA WITH FISH SAUCES

•

PASTA & VEGETABLE DISHES

2

PASTA DISHES

CHAPTER SIX

First Courses

Pasta dishes perfectly fulfil the requirements of an opening course – to give family and friends an immediate feeling of well-being, to delight the eye and excite the palate. This is the time to serve clear but hearty soups contrasting the colours, textures and flavours of crisp, fresh vegetables and short pasta shapes; for a burst of mingled flavours such as those of roasted vegetables or spicy sausage, and for subtle, creamy sauces with herbs and nuts.

Serve the first course in the prettiest dishes you have, in scallop shells, or on glass plates. Serve hot dishes piping hot, cold ones refreshingly, tinglingly cold. Garnish each one with a leaf or a sprig or two of herbs, and serve them with a choice of breads in the Mediterranean style: long, crisp grissini breadsticks, olive ciabatta bread or warm Italian loaves.

Opposite: *An Italian fisherman and his wife inspect the nets. A wide variety of fish and shellfish are caught in the seas around the Italian coast, and this abundance is reflected in the antipasti, which often include fish soups and seafood salads.*

HARICOT BEAN & PASTA SOUP

A dish with proud Mediterranean origins, this soup is a winter warmer, to be served with warm, crusty bread and, if you like, a slice of cheese.

STEP 1

STEP 2

STEP 3

STEP 4

SERVES 4

250 g/8 oz/generous 1 cup dried haricot beans, soaked, drained and rinsed (see below)
4 tbsp olive oil
2 large onions, sliced
3 garlic cloves, chopped
425 g/15 oz can chopped tomatoes
1 tsp dried oregano
1 tsp tomato purée (paste)
900 ml/1¹/₂ pints/3¹/₂ cups water
90 g/3 oz small pasta shapes, such as fusilli or conchigliette
125 g/4 oz sun-dried tomatoes in oil, drained and sliced thinly
1 tbsp chopped fresh coriander (cilantro) or flat-leaf parsley
2 tbsp grated Parmesan cheese
salt and pepper

1 Put the soaked beans into a large pan, cover with cold water and bring them to the boil. Boil rapidly for 15 minutes to remove any harmful toxins. Drain the beans in a colander.

2 Heat the oil in a pan over a medium heat and fry the onions until they are just beginning to change colour. Stir in the garlic and cook for 1 further minute. Stir in the chopped tomatoes, oregano and the tomato purée (paste) and pour on the water. Add the beans, bring to the boil and cover the pan. Simmer for 45 minutes or until the beans are almost tender.

3 Add the pasta, season the soup and stir in the sun-dried tomatoes. Return the soup to the boil, partly cover the pan and continue boiling for 10 minutes until the pasta is nearly tender.

4 Stir in the chopped herb. Taste the soup and adjust the seasoning if necessary. Transfer to a warmed soup tureen to serve, sprinkled with the Parmesan cheese. Serve hot.

DRIED BEANS

You can soak the dried beans for several hours or overnight in a large bowl of cold water, or, if it is more convenient, place them in a pan of cold water and bring them to the boil. Remove the pan from the heat and leave the beans to cool in the water. Drain and rinse the beans before beginning the recipe.

STEP 2

STEP 3

STEP 4

STEP 5

CHICKEN SCALLOPS

Served in scallop shells, this makes a stylish presentation for a dinner-party first course.

SERVES 4

175 g/6 oz short-cut macaroni or other
*   short pasta shapes*
3 tbsp vegetable oil, plus extra for brushing
1 onion, chopped finely
3 slices unsmoked collar or back bacon, rinds
*   removed and chopped*
125 g/4 oz button mushrooms, sliced thinly
*   or chopped*
175 g/6 oz/³/₄ cup cooked chicken, diced
175 ml/6 fl oz/³/₄ cup crème fraîche
4 tbsp dry breadcrumbs
60 g/2 oz/¹/₂ cup Cheddar cheese, grated
salt and pepper
fresh flat-leaf parsley sprigs, to garnish

1 Cook the pasta in a large pan of boiling salted water, adding 1 tablespoon of the oil. When the pasta is almost tender, drain in a colander. Return to the pan and cover.

2 Heat the grill (broiler) to medium. Heat the remaining oil in a pan over medium heat and fry the onion until it is translucent. Add the chopped bacon and mushrooms and cook for a further 3–4 minutes, stirring once or twice.

3 Stir in the pasta, chicken and crème fraîche and season.

4 Brush 4 large scallop shells with oil. Spoon in the chicken mixture and smooth to make neat mounds.

5 Mix together the breadcrumbs and cheese and sprinkle over the top of the chicken mixture. Press the topping lightly into the chicken mixture, then grill (broil) for 4–5 minutes until golden brown and bubbling. Garnish with parsley, and serve hot.

VARIATION

If you do not have scallop shells, you can assemble this dish in four small ovenproof dishes, such as ramekins, or in one large one. Look in good kitchen supply stores for ovenproof scallop-shaped dishes.

SPICY SAUSAGE SALAD

A warm sausage and pasta dressing spooned over chilled salad leaves makes a refreshing combination to start a meal with.

STEP 1

STEP 2

STEP 3

STEP 4

SERVES 4

125 g/4 oz small pasta shapes, such as
  elbow tubetti
3 tbsp olive oil
1 onion, chopped
2 cloves garlic, crushed
1 small yellow (bell) pepper, cored, deseeded
  and cut into julienne strips
175 g/6 oz spicy pork sausage, such as
  pepperoni, skinned and sliced
2 tbsp red wine
1 tbsp red wine vinegar
mixed salad leaves, chilled
salt

1 Cook the pasta in a large pan of boiling salted water, adding 1 tablespoon of the oil. When almost tender, drain it in a colander and set aside.

2 Heat the remaining oil in a saucepan over a medium heat. Fry the onion until translucent, stir in the garlic, (bell) pepper and sausage and cook for 3–4 minutes, stirring once or twice.

3 Add the wine, wine vinegar and reserved pasta to the pan, stir to blend well and bring the mixture just to the boil.

4 Arrange the chilled salad leaves on 4 individual serving plates and spoon on the warm sausage and pasta mixture. Serve at once.

SPICED SAUSAGES

Italian pepperoni, flavoured with chilli peppers, fennel and spices, is an ideal sausage to use for this recipe. Alternatively, try one of the many varieties of salami, usually flavoured with garlic and pepper.

STEP 1

STEP 2

STEP 2

STEP 3

SPAGHETTI WITH RICOTTA CHEESE

This makes a quick and easy first course, ideal for the summer.

SERVES 4

350 g/12 oz spaghetti
3 tbsp olive oil
45 g/1½ oz/3 tbsp butter, cut into small
*   pieces*
2 tbsp fresh chopped flat-leaf parsley
salt

SAUCE:
125 g/4 oz/1 cup freshly ground almonds
125 g/4 oz/½ cup Ricotta cheese
large pinch grated nutmeg
large pinch ground cinnamon
150 ml/¼ pint/⅔ cup crème fraîche
120 ml/4 fl oz/½ cup hot chicken stock
pepper
1 tbsp pine kernels (nuts)
fresh coriander (cilantro) leaves, to garnish

1 Cook the spaghetti in a large pan of boiling salted water, adding 1 tablespoon of the oil. When it is almost tender, drain the pasta in a colander. Return it to the pan and toss with the butter and parsley. Cover the pan and keep warm.

2 To make the sauce, mix together the ground almonds, Ricotta, nutmeg, cinnamon and crème fraîche to make a thick paste. Gradually pour in the remaining oil, stirring constantly until it is well blended. Gradually pour in the hot stock, stirring all the time, until the sauce is smooth. Season with pepper.

3 Transfer the spaghetti to a warmed serving dish, pour on the sauce and toss well. Sprinkle each serving with pine kernels (nuts) and garnish with fresh coriander (cilantro) leaves. Serve warm.

TOSSING SPAGHETTI

To toss spaghetti and coat it thoroughly with a sauce or dressing, use the 2 largest forks you can find – special forks are sold in some kitchen stores just for this purpose. Holding one fork in each hand, ease the prongs under the spaghetti from each side and lift them towards the centre. Repeat evenly and rhythmically until the pasta is well and truly tossed.

STEP 2

STEP 2

STEP 2

STEP 3

CHILLED NOODLES & (BELL) PEPPERS

This is a convenient dish to serve when you are arriving home just before family or friends. You can have it all prepared ahead, ready to assemble in minutes.

SERVES 4–6

*250 g/8 oz ribbon noodles, or Chinese egg
   noodles
1 tbsp sesame oil
1 red (bell)pepper
1 yellow (bell) pepper
1 green (bell) pepper
6 spring onions (scallions), cut into
   julienne strips
salt*

*DRESSING:
5 tbsp sesame oil
2 tbsp light soy sauce
1 tbsp tahini (sesame paste)
4–5 drops hot pepper sauce*

1 Preheat the grill (broiler) to medium. Cook the noodles in a large pan of boiling salted water until they are almost tender. Drain them in a colander, run cold water through them and drain thoroughly. Tip the noodles into a bowl, stir in the sesame oil, cover and chill.

2 Cook the (bell) peppers under the grill (broiler), turning them frequently, until they are blackened on all sides. Plunge into cold water, then skin them. Cut in half, remove the cores and seeds and cut the flesh into thick strips. Set aside in a covered container.

3 To make the dressing, mix together the sesame oil, soy sauce, tahini and hot pepper sauce.

4 Pour the dressing on to the noodles, reserving 1 tablespoon, and toss well. Turn the noodles into a serving dish, arrange the (bell) peppers over the noodles and spoon on the reserved dressing. Scatter on the spring onion (scallion) strips.

VARIATION

If you have time, another way of skinning (bell) peppers is to first grill (broil) them, then place in a plastic bag, seal and leave for about 20 minutes. The skin will then peel off easily.

VEGETABLE & PASTA SALAD

Roasted vegetables and pasta make a delicious, colourful salad, ideal as a first course or to serve with a platter of cold meats.

SERVES 4
OVEN: 220°C/425°F/GAS MARK 7

2 small aubergines (eggplants), sliced thinly
1 large onion, sliced
2 large beef-steak tomatoes, skinned and cut
into wedges
1 red (bell) pepper, cored, deseeded and
sliced
1 fennel bulb, sliced thinly
2 garlic cloves, sliced
4 tbsp olive oil
175 g/6 oz small pasta shapes, such as stars
salad leaves
90 g/3 oz/¹/₂ cup feta cheese, crumbled
a few basil leaves, torn
salt and pepper

DRESSING:
5 tbsp olive oil
juice of 1 orange
1 tsp grated orange rind
¹/₄ tsp paprika
4 canned anchovies, chopped finely

1 Place the sliced aubergines (eggplants) in a colander, sprinkle with salt and leave for about 1 hour for the salt to draw out the bitter juices. Rinse under cold running water to remove the salt, then drain. Dry on paper towels.

2 Arrange the aubergines (eggplants), onion, tomatoes, red (bell) pepper, fennel and garlic in a single layer in an ovenproof dish, sprinkle on 3 tablespoons of the olive oil and season with salt and pepper. Bake in a preheated oven, uncovered, for 45 minutes, until the vegetables begin to turn brown. Remove from the oven and set aside to cool.

3 Cook the pasta in a large pan of boiling salted water, adding the remaining olive oil. When the pasta is almost tender, drain it in a colander, then transfer it to a bowl.

4 To make the dressing, mix together the olive oil, orange juice, orange rind and paprika. Stir in the finely chopped anchovies and season with pepper. Pour the dressing over the pasta while it is still hot, and toss well. Set the pasta aside to cool.

5 To assemble the salad, line a shallow serving dish with the salad leaves and arrange the cold roasted vegetables in the centre. Spoon the pasta in a ring around the vegetables and scatter over the feta cheese and basil leaves. Serve at once.

CHAPTER SEVEN

Pasta with Meat Sauces

Some of the most popular and best-known pasta dishes are ones
that bring together long strands of pasta cooked *al dente*,
and a rich, hearty sauce including beef or lamb, chicken or ham.
Spaghetti Bolognese needs no introduction, and yet it is said
that there are almost as many versions of this delicious regional
dish as there are lovers of Italian food. Our version includes both
beef and bacon in a sauce enriched with beef stock and red wine.

Layered pasta dishes that are served in slices, wedges or squares are
perfect standbys for parties and picnics, buffet meals or informal
family occasions; children and teenagers love them. Our selection
includes creamy lasagne and pasticcio, an aubergine (eggplant)
and pasta cake, and an unusual meat loaf with a contrasting pasta
layer; they will all make worthy additions to your repertoire of
baked pasta favourites.

*Opposite: Verdant landscape
near Bologna, home of some
splendid hams, as well as one of
the best-known pasta sauces –
Bolognese.*

SPAGHETTI CARBONARA

Have all the cooked ingredients as hot as possible, so that the beaten eggs are cooked on contact. This is a classic dish, and one to serve with a flourish.

STEP 1

SERVES 4

400 g/14 oz spaghetti
2 tbsp olive oil
1 large onion, sliced thinly
2 garlic cloves, chopped
175 g/6 oz streaky bacon slices, rinds removed and cut into thin strips
30 g/1 oz/2 tbsp butter
175 g/6 oz mushrooms, sliced thinly
300 ml/¹/₂ pint/1¹/₄ cups double (heavy) cream
3 eggs, beaten
90 g/3 oz/³/₄ cup Parmesan cheese, grated, plus extra to serve (optional)
salt and pepper
fresh sage sprigs, to garnish

1 Heat a large serving dish or bowl. Cook the spaghetti in a large pan of boiling salted water, adding 1 tablespoon of the oil. When the pasta is almost tender, drain it in a colander. Return the spaghetti to the pan, cover and leave it in a warm place.

2 While the spaghetti is cooking, heat the remaining oil in a frying pan (skillet) over a medium heat. Fry the onion until it is translucent, then add the garlic and bacon and continue frying until the bacon is crisp.

3 Remove the onion, garlic and bacon with a perforated spoon and set it aside to keep warm. Heat the butter in the pan and fry the mushrooms for 3–4 minutes, stirring them once or twice. Return the bacon mixture to the mushrooms. Cover and keep warm.

4 Stir together the cream, the beaten eggs and Parmesan cheese and season with salt and pepper.

5 Working very quickly to avoid cooling the cooked ingredients, tip the spaghetti into the bacon and mushroom mixture and pour on the eggs. Toss the spaghetti quickly, using 2 forks, and serve it at once. You can, if you wish, hand round more grated Parmesan.

STEP 3

STEP 4

ACCOMPANIMENTS

A chilled salad of mixed leaves such as young spinach, radicchio and endive (chicory) tossed in a vinaigrette dressing makes a good accompaniment. You may also like to serve a bowl of chilled radishes.

STEP 5

SPAGHETTI BOLOGNESE

This familiar meat sauce, also known as ragù sauce, can be used in lasagne, and in other baked dishes as well. It is so versatile that it is a good idea to make it in large quantities, and freeze some.

STEP 1

STEP 2

STEP 3

STEP 4

SERVES 4

400 g/14 oz spaghetti
1 tbsp olive oil
salt
15 g/¹/₂ oz/1 tbsp butter
2 tbsp chopped fresh parsley, to garnish

RAGU SAUCE:
3 tbsp olive oil
45 g/1¹/₂ oz/3 tbsp butter
2 large onions, chopped
4 celery sticks, sliced thinly
175 g/6 oz streaky bacon, chopped into
*   small strips*
2 garlic cloves, chopped
500 g/1 lb lean beef, minced (ground)
2 tbsp tomato purée (paste)
1 tbsp plain (all-purpose) flour
425 g/15 oz can chopped tomatoes
150 ml/¹/₄ pint/²/₃ cup beef stock
150 ml/¹/₄ pint/²/₃ cup red wine
2 tsp dried oregano
¹/₂ tsp grated nutmeg
salt and pepper

1 To make the ragù sauce: heat the oil and the butter in a large frying pan (skillet) over a medium heat. Add the onions, celery and bacon pieces and fry them together for 5 minutes, stirring once or twice.

2 Stir in the garlic and minced (ground) beef and cook, stirring, until the meat has lost its redness. Lower the heat and continue cooking for a further 10 minutes, stirring occasionally.

3 Increase the heat to medium, stir in the tomato purée (paste) and the flour and cook for 1–2 minutes. Stir in the chopped tomatoes and the beef stock and wine and bring to the boil, stirring. Season the sauce and stir in the oregano and nutmeg. Cover the pan and simmer for 45 minutes, stirring occasionally.

4 Cook the spaghetti in a large pan of boiling salted water, adding the olive oil. When it is almost tender, drain it in a colander, then return to the pan. Dot the spaghetti with the butter and toss thoroughly.

5 Taste the sauce and adjust the seasoning if necessary. Pour the sauce over the spaghetti and toss well. Sprinkle on the parsley to garnish and serve immediately.

STUFFED CANNELLONI

Cannelloni, the thick round pasta tubes, make perfect containers for close-textured sauces of all kinds.

STEP 1

STEP 2

STEP 4

STEP 5

SERVES 4
OVEN: 190°C/375°F/GAS MARK 5

8 cannelloni tubes
1 tbsp olive oil
fresh herbs, to garnish

FILLING:
30 g/1 oz/2 tbsp butter
300 g/10 oz frozen spinach, defrosted and
  chopped
125 g/4 oz /¹/₂ cup Ricotta cheese
30 g/1 oz/¹/₄ cup Parmesan cheese, grated
60 g/2 oz/¹/₄ cup chopped ham
¹/₄ tsp grated nutmeg
2 tbsp double (heavy) cream
2 eggs, lightly beaten
salt and pepper

SAUCE:
30 g/1 oz/2 tbsp butter
30 g/1 oz/¹/₄ cup plain (all-purpose) flour
300 ml/¹/₂ pint/1¹/₄ cups milk
2 bay leaves
large pinch grated nutmeg
30 g/1 oz /¹/₄ cup Parmesan, grated

1 To prepare the filling, melt the butter in a pan and stir in the spinach. Stir for 2–3 minutes to allow the moisture to evaporate, then remove the pan from the heat. Stir in the cheeses and the ham. Season with nutmeg, salt and pepper and beat in the cream and eggs to make a thick paste. Set aside to cool.

2 Cook the cannelloni in a large pan of boiling salted water, adding the olive oil. When almost tender, after 10–12 minutes, drain it in a colander and set aside to cool.

3 To make the sauce, melt the butter in a pan, stir in the flour and, when it has formed a roux, gradually pour on the milk, stirring all the time. Add the bay leaves, bring to simmering point, and cook for 5 minutes. Season with nutmeg, salt and pepper. Remove the pan from the heat and discard the bay leaves.

4 To assemble the dish, spoon the filling into a piping bag. Pipe it into each of the cannelloni tubes.

5 Spoon a little of the sauce into a shallow baking dish. Arrange the cannelloni in a single layer, then pour over the remaining sauce. Sprinkle on the remaining Parmesan cheese and bake in a preheated oven for 40–45 minutes until the sauce is golden brown and bubbling. Serve garnished with fresh herb sprigs.

LASAGNE VERDE

*The sauce in this delicious baked pasta dish is the same sauce
that is served with Spaghetti Bolognese (see page 102).*

SERVES 6
OVEN: 190°C/375°F/GAS MARK 5

1 quantity Ragù Sauce (see page 102)
1 tbsp olive oil
250 g/8 oz lasagne verde
*1 quantity Béchamel Sauce (see
   page 232)*
60 g/2 oz/¹/₂ cup Parmesan, grated
salt and pepper
salad or black olives, to serve

1 Begin by making the ragù sauce
as described on page 102. Cook
the sauce for 10–12 minutes longer
than the time given, in an uncovered
pan, to allow the excess liquid to
evaporate. To layer the sauce with
lasagne, it needs to be reduced until it
has the consistency of a thick paste.

2 Have ready a large pan of boiling
salted water and add the olive oil.
Drop the pasta sheets into the boiling
water, 2 or 3 at a time, and return the
water to the boil before adding further
pasta sheets. If you are using fresh
lasagne, cook the sheets for a total of
8 minutes. If you are using dried or
partly precooked pasta, cook it
according to the directions given on the
packet.

3 Spread a large, dampened tea towel
(dish cloth) on a work surface
(counter). Lift out the pasta sheets with a
perforated spoon and spread them in a
single layer on the tea towel (dish cloth).
Use a second tea towel (dish cloth) if
necessary. Set the pasta aside while you
make the béchamel sauce, as described
on page 232.

4 Grease a rectangular ovenproof
dish, about 25–28 cm/10–11
inches long. To assemble the dish, spoon
a little of the meat sauce into the
prepared dish, cover with a layer of
lasagne, then spoon over a little
béchamel sauce and sprinkle on a little
cheese. Continue making layers in this
way, covering the final layer of lasagne
with the remaining béchamel sauce.

5 Sprinkle on the remaining cheese
and bake in a preheated oven for
40 minutes until the sauce is golden
brown and bubbling. Serve with a chilled
green salad, a tomato salad, or a bowl of
black olives.

TAGLIATELLE WITH CHICKEN

Spinach ribbon noodles covered with a rich tomato sauce and topped with creamy chicken make a very appetizing dish.

STEP 1

SERVES 4

250 g/8 oz fresh green ribbon noodles
1 tbsp olive oil
salt
1 quantity Tomato Sauce (see page 163)
basil leaves, to garnish

CHICKEN SAUCE:
60 g/2 oz/¹/₄ cup unsalted butter
400 g/14 oz boned, skinned chicken breast,
* sliced thinly*
90 g/3 oz/³/₄ cup blanched almonds
300 ml/¹/₂ pint/1¹/₄ cups double (heavy)
* cream*
salt and pepper

1 Make the tomato sauce as described on page 163, then set aside and keep warm.

2 To make the chicken sauce, melt the butter in a pan over a medium heat and fry the chicken strips and almonds for 5–6 minutes, stirring frequently, until the chicken is cooked through.

3 Meanwhile, pour the cream into a small pan over a low heat, bring it to the boil and boil for about 10 minutes, until reduced by almost half. Pour the

STEP 1

cream over the chicken and almonds, stir well, and season. Set it aside and keep it warm.

4 Cook the fresh pasta in a large pan of boiling salted water, adding the oil. When the pasta is just tender, about 5 minutes, drain it in a colander, then return it to the pan, cover and keep it warm.

5 To assemble the dish, turn the pasta into a warmed serving dish and spoon the tomato sauce over it. Spoon the chicken and cream over the centre, scatter the basil leaves over and serve at once.

STEP 2

TOMATO SAUCE

This tomato sauce can be served with a variety of pasta dishes. Make double the quantity and keep some in the freezer to make a useful standby for quick and easy pasta dishes.

STEP 3

LAYERED MEAT LOAF

*A cheesy pasta layer comes as a pleasant surprise inside
this lightly spiced meat loaf.*

STEP 2

STEP 5

STEP 5

STEP 6

SERVES 6
OVEN: 180°C/350°F/GAS MARK 4

30 g/1 oz/2 tbsp butter, plus extra for
    greasing
1 onion, chopped finely
1 small red (bell) pepper, cored, deseeded and
    chopped
1 garlic clove, chopped
500 g/1 lb lean beef, minced (ground)
30 g/1 oz/¹/₂ cup soft white breadcrumbs
¹/₂ tsp chopped chilli pepper
1 tbsp lemon juice
¹/₂ tsp grated lemon rind
2 tbsp chopped fresh flat-leaf parsley
90 g/3 oz short pasta, such as fusilli
1 tbsp olive oil
1 quantity Cheese Sauce (see pages 228–9)
4 bay leaves
175 g/6 oz streaky bacon slices, rinds
    removed
salt and pepper
salad leaves, to garnish

1 Melt the butter in a pan over a medium heat and fry the onion and (bell) pepper for about 3 minutes, until the onion is translucent. Stir in the garlic and cook for a further 1 minute.

2 Put the meat into a large bowl and mash it with a wooden spoon until it becomes a sticky paste. Tip in the fried vegetables and stir in the breadcrumbs, chilli pepper, lemon juice, lemon rind and parsley. Season the mixture with salt and pepper and set it aside.

3 Cook the pasta in a large pan of boiling salted water, adding the olive oil. When it is almost tender, drain it in a colander.

4 Make the Cheese Sauce as described on pages 228–9. Stir in the pasta.

5 Grease a 1 kg/2 lb loaf tin (pan) and arrange the bay leaves in the base. Stretch the bacon slices with the back of a knife blade and arrange them to line the base and sides of the tin (pan). Spoon in half the meat mixture, level the surface and cover with the pasta. Spoon in the remaining meat mixture, level the top and cover the tin (pan) with foil.

6 Cook in a preheated oven for 1 hour or until the juices run clear and the loaf has shrunk from the sides. Pour off any excess fat from the tin (pan) and turn the loaf out on to a warmed serving dish. Serve hot, garnished with salad leaves.

AUBERGINE (EGGPLANT) CAKE

Layers of toasty-brown aubergine (eggplant), meat sauce and cheese-flavoured pasta make this a popular family supper dish.

STEP 2

STEP 3

STEP 5

STEP 6

SERVES 4
OVEN: 190°C/375°F/GAS MARK 5

1 aubergine (eggplant), sliced thinly
5 tbsp olive oil
1 quantity Lamb Sauce (see page 229)
250 g/8 oz short pasta shapes, such as fusilli
60 g/2 oz/¼ cup butter, plus extra for
  greasing
45 g/1½ oz/6 tbsp plain (all-purpose) flour
300 ml/½ pint/1¼ cups milk
150ml/¼ pint/⅔ cup single (light) cream
150 ml/¼ pint/⅔ cup chicken stock
large pinch grated nutmeg
90 g/3 oz/¾ cup Cheddar cheese, grated
30 g/1 oz/¼ cup Parmesan cheese, grated
salt and pepper

1 Put the aubergine (eggplant) slices in a colander, sprinkle with salt and leave for about 45 minutes while the salt draws out some of the bitter juices. Rinse the aubergine (eggplant) under cold running water and drain. Toss in paper towels to dry.

2 Heat 4 tablespoons of the oil in a frying pan (skillet) over a medium heat. Fry the aubergine (eggplant) slices for about 4 minutes on each side, until light golden. Remove with a perforated spoon and drain on paper towels.

3 Make the lamb sauce as described on page 229 and keep warm.

4 Meanwhile, cook the pasta in a large pan of boiling salted water, adding 1 tablespoon of olive oil. When the pasta is almost tender, drain it in a colander and return to the pan. Cover and keep warm.

5 Melt the butter in a small pan, stir in the flour and cook for 1 minute. Gradually pour on the milk, stirring all the time, then stir in the cream and chicken stock. Season with nutmeg, salt and pepper, bring to the boil and simmer for 5 minutes. Stir in the Cheddar and remove the pan from the heat. Pour half the sauce over the pasta and mix well. Reserve the remaining sauce.

6 Grease a shallow ovenproof dish. Spoon in half the pasta, cover it with half the lamb sauce and then with the aubergine (eggplant) in a single layer. Repeat the layers of pasta and meat sauce and spread the remaining cheese sauce over the top. Sprinkle on the Parmesan. Bake in a preheated oven for 25 minutes, until the top is golden brown. Serve hot or cold, with an artichoke heart and tomato salad.

PASTICCIO

A recipe that has both Italian and Greek origins, this dish may be served hot or cold, cut into thick, satisfying squares.

SERVES 6
OVEN: 190°C/375°F/GAS MARK 5

250 g/8 oz fusilli, or other short pasta
 shapes
1 tbsp olive oil
4 tbsp double (heavy) cream
salt
fresh rosemary sprigs, to garnish

SAUCE:
2 tbsp olive oil, plus extra for brushing
1 onion, sliced thinly
1 red (bell) pepper, cored, deseeded and
 chopped
2 garlic cloves, chopped
625 g/1¼ lb lean beef, minced (ground)
425 g/15 oz can chopped tomatoes
125 ml/4 fl oz/½ cup dry white wine
2 tbsp chopped fresh flat-leaf parsley
50 g/2 oz can anchovies, drained and
 chopped
salt and pepper

TOPPING:
300 ml/½ pint/1¼ cups natural yogurt
3 eggs
pinch grated nutmeg
45 g/1½ oz/⅓ cup Parmesan cheese, grated

1 To make the sauce, heat the oil in a large frying pan (skillet) and fry the onion and red (bell) pepper for 3 minutes. Stir in the garlic and cook for 1 minute more. Stir in the beef and cook, stirring frequently, until it has changed colour.

2 Add the tomatoes and wine, stir well and bring to the boil. Simmer, uncovered, for 20 minutes until the sauce is fairly thick. Stir in the parsley and anchovies and adjust the seasoning.

3 Cook the pasta in a large pan of boiling salted water, adding the oil. When it is almost tender, drain it in a colander, then transfer it to a bowl. Stir in the cream and set it aside.

4 To make the topping, beat together the yogurt, eggs, nutmeg and salt and pepper. Stir in half the cheese.

5 Brush a shallow baking dish with oil. Spoon in half the pasta and cover with half the meat sauce. Repeat these layers, spread the topping over evenly and sprinkle on remaining cheese.

6 Bake in a preheated oven for 25 minutes until the topping is golden brown and bubbling. Garnish with rosemary and serve with a selection of raw vegetable crudités.

STEP 1

STEP 2

STEP 4

STEP 5

TAGLIATELLE WITH MEATBALLS

There is an appetizing contrast of textures and flavours in this satisfying family dish.

STEP 1

STEP 2

STEP 2

STEP 3

SERVES 4

500 g/1 lb lean beef, minced (ground)
60 g/2 oz/1 cup soft white breadcrumbs
1 garlic clove, crushed
2 tbsp chopped fresh flat-leaf parsley
1 tsp dried oregano
large pinch grated nutmeg
¼ tsp ground coriander
60 g/2 oz/½ cup Parmesan cheese, grated
2–3 tbsp milk
plain (all-purpose) flour for dusting
4 tbsp olive oil
400 g/14 oz tagliatelle
30 g/1 oz/2 tbsp butter, diced
salt
2 tbsp chopped flat-leaf parsley, to garnish

SAUCE:
3 tbsp olive oil
2 large onions, sliced
2 celery sticks, sliced thinly
2 garlic cloves, chopped
425 g/15 oz can chopped tomatoes
125 g/4 oz sun-dried tomatoes in oil,
*   drained and chopped*
2 tbsp tomato purée (paste)
1 tbsp dark Muscovado sugar
150 ml/¼ pint/⅔ cup white wine or water
salt and pepper

1 To make the sauce, heat the oil in a frying pan (skillet) and fry the onion and celery until translucent. Add the garlic and cook for 1 minute. Stir in the tomatoes, tomato purée (paste), sugar and wine and season. Bring to the boil and simmer for 10 minutes.

2 Break up the meat in a bowl with a wooden spoon until it becomes a sticky paste. Stir in the breadcrumbs, garlic, herbs and spices. Stir in the cheese and enough milk to make a firm paste. Flour your hands, and shape the mixture into 12 balls. Heat 3 tablespoons of the oil in a pan and fry the meatballs for 5–6 minutes until browned.

3 Pour the tomato sauce over the meatballs. Lower the heat, cover the pan and simmer for 30 minutes, turning once or twice. Add a little extra water if the sauce begins to dry.

4 Cook the pasta in a large saucepan of boiling salted water, adding the remaining oil. When almost tender, drain it, then turn into a warmed serving dish, dot with the butter and toss with 2 forks. Spoon the meatballs and sauce over the pasta and sprinkle on the parsley. Serve with a green salad.

CHAPTER EIGHT

Pasta with Fish Sauces

Macaroni with mushrooms and prawns (shrimp) or calamares; wholewheat lasagne with smoked fish and prawns (shrimp); pasta shells with mussels; spaghetti with smoked salmon or with anchovies and tuna; vermicelli with clams – these are irresistible combinations that have a whiff of the sea and, in most cases, the flavour of the Mediterranean.

These dishes are as practical as they are delicious, all perfect choices for the busy cook who has to keep an eye on the clock. In general, since fish and shellfish need only the briefest of cooking times, the sauce and the pasta can be ready together, perfectly cooked and perfectly timed just as the family is assembling or the guests are arriving.

Opposite: *Open-air restaurant beside Lake Garda. The many rivers and lakes in Italy are a rich source of fish and shellfish, which feature largely in pasta sauces.*

SPAGHETTI WITH SEAFOOD SAUCE

Frozen peeled prawns (shrimp) from the freezer can become the star ingredient in this colourful and tasty dish.

STEP 2

SERVES 4

250 g/8 oz spaghetti, broken into 15 cm/ 6 inch lengths
2 tbsp olive oil
300 ml/½ pint/1¼ cups chicken stock
1 tsp lemon juice
1 small cauliflower, cut into florets
2 carrots, sliced thinly
125 g/4 oz mangetout (snow peas), trimmed
60 g/2 oz/¼ cup butter
1 onion, sliced
250 g/8 oz courgettes (zucchini), sliced thinly
1 garlic clove, chopped
350 g/12 oz frozen peeled prawns (shrimp), defrosted
2 tbsp chopped fresh flat-leaf parsley
30 g/1 oz/¼ cup Parmesan cheese, grated
salt and pepper
½ tsp paprika, to sprinkle
4 unpeeled prawns (shrimp), to garnish (optional)

1 Cook the spaghetti in a large pan of boiling salted water, adding 1 tablespoon of the olive oil. When it is almost tender, drain it in a colander. Return to the pan and stir in the remaining olive oil. Cover the pan and keep warm.

2 Bring the chicken stock and lemon juice to the boil in a pan over a medium heat and cook the cauliflower and carrots for 3–4 minutes until they are barely tender. Remove with a perforated spoon and set aside. Add the mangetout (snow peas) to the stock and cook for 3–4 minutes, until they begin to soften. Remove with a perforated spoon and add to the other vegetables. Reserve the stock for future use.

STEP 3

3 Melt half the butter in a frying pan (skillet) over a medium heat and fry the onion and courgettes (zucchini) for about 3 minutes. Add the garlic and prawns (shrimp)and cook for a further 2–3 minutes until they are thoroughly heated through.

STEP 3

4 Stir in the reserved vegetables and season well. When the vegetables are heated through add the remaining butter, stirring until melted.

5 Transfer the spaghetti to a warmed serving dish. Pour on the sauce and parsley and toss well, using 2 forks, until thoroughly coated. Sprinkle on the grated cheese and paprika and garnish with prawns (shrimp), if using. Serve immediately.

STEP 4

STEP 2

STEP 3

STEP 4

STEP 4

MACARONI & PRAWN (SHRIMP) BAKE

This adaptation of an 18th-century Italian dish is baked until it is golden brown and sizzling, then cut into wedges, like a cake.

SERVES 4
OVEN: 180°C/350°F/GAS MARK 4

350 g/12 oz short pasta, such as short-cut
  macaroni
1 tbsp olive oil, plus extra for brushing
90 g/3 oz/6 tbsp butter, plus extra for
  greasing
2 small fennel bulbs, sliced thinly, leaves
  reserved
175 g/6 oz mushrooms, sliced thinly
175 g/6 oz peeled prawns (shrimp)
Béchamel Sauce (see page 228)
pinch chilli powder
60 g/2 oz/¹/₂ cup Parmesan cheese, grated
2 large tomatoes, sliced
1 tsp dried oregano
salt and pepper

1 Cook the pasta in a large pan of boiling salted water, adding 1 tablespoon of olive oil. When the pasta is almost tender, drain it in a colander, return to the pan and dot with 30g/ 1 oz/2 tablespoons of the butter. Shake the pan well, cover tightly and keep the pasta warm.

2 Melt the remaining butter in a pan over a medium heat and fry the fennel for 3–4 minutes until it begins to soften. Stir in the mushrooms and fry for

a further 2 minutes. Stir in the prawns (shrimp), remove the pan from the heat and set it aside.

3 Make the béchamel sauce and add the chilli powder. Remove the pan from the heat and stir in the reserved vegetables and prawns (shrimp) and the pasta.

4 Grease a round, shallow ovenproof dish. Pour in the pasta mixture and spread it out evenly. Sprinkle on the Parmesan and arrange the tomato slices in a ring around the edge of the dish. Brush the tomato with olive oil and sprinkle on the dried oregano.

5 Bake in a preheated oven for 25 minutes, until the top is golden brown. Serve hot.

ACCOMPANIMENT

A mixed green salad, tossed with the reserved fennel leaves and sprinkled with crumbled feta cheese, goes well with this dish.

SEAFOOD LASAGNE

Layers of cheese sauce, smoked cod and wholemeal lasagne can be assembled in advance and left ready to cook on the following day.

STEP 2

SERVES 6

OVEN: 190°C/375°F/GAS MARK 5

8 sheets wholewheat lasagne
500 g/ 1 lb smoked cod
600 ml/ 1 pint/ 2½ cups milk
1 tbsp lemon juice
8 peppercorns
2 bay leaves
a few sprigs fresh flat-leaf parsley
60 g/ 2 oz/ ½ cup Cheddar cheese, grated
30 g/ 1 oz/ ¼ cup Parmesan cheese, grated
salt and pepper
a few whole prawns (shrimp), to garnish
   (optional)

SAUCE:
60 g/ 2 oz/ ¼ cup butter, plus extra for
   greasing
1 large onion, sliced
1 green (bell) pepper, cored, deseeded and
   chopped
1 small courgette (zucchini), sliced
60 g/ 2 oz/ ½ cup plain (all-purpose) flour
150 ml/ ¼ pint/ ⅔ cup white wine
150 ml/ ¼ pint/ ⅔ cup single (light) cream
125 g/ 4 oz peeled prawns (shrimp)
60 g/ 2 oz/ ½ cup Cheddar cheese, grated

1 Cook the lasagne in boiling salted water until almost tender. Drain in a colander and reserve.

2 Place the smoked cod, milk, lemon juice, peppercorns, bay leaves and parsley in a frying pan (skillet). Bring to the boil, cover and simmer for 10 minutes.

STEP 4

3 Remove the fish, skin it and remove any bones. Flake the fish. Strain and reserve the liquid.

4 Make the sauce: melt the butter and fry the onion, (bell) pepper and courgette (zucchini) for 2–3 minutes. Stir in the flour and cook for 1 minute. Gradually add the fish liquid, then stir in the wine, cream and prawns (shrimp). Simmer for 2 minutes. Remove from the heat, add the cheese, and season.

STEP 5

5 Grease a shallow ovenproof dish. Pour in a quarter of the sauce and spread over the base. Cover the sauce with 3 sheets of lasagne, then with another quarter of the sauce. Arrange the fish on top, then cover with half the remaining sauce. Add the remaining lasagne, then remaining sauce. Sprinkle the Cheddar and Parmesan over.

6 Bake in a preheated oven for 25 minutes, or until the top is golden brown and bubbling. Garnish with a few whole prawns (shrimp), if liked.

STEP 5

STEP 1

STEP 2

STEP 3

STEP 5

PASTA SHELLS WITH MUSSELS

Serve this aromatic seafood dish to family and friends who admit to a love of garlic!

SERVES 4–6

400 g/14 oz pasta shells
1 tbsp olive oil

SAUCE:
3.5 litres/6 pints mussels, scrubbed
2 large onions, chopped
250 ml/8 fl oz/1 cup dry white wine
125 g/4 oz/½ cup unsalted butter
6 large garlic cloves, chopped finely
5 tbsp chopped fresh flat-leaf parsley
300 ml/½ pint/1¼ cups double (heavy)
*   cream*
salt and pepper

1 Pull off the 'beards' from the mussels and rinse the mussels well in several changes of water, discarding any that refuse to close when tapped. Put the mussels in a large pan with one of the onions and the white wine. Cover the pan, shake and cook over a medium heat for 2–3 minutes until the mussels open.

2 Remove the pan from the heat, lift out the mussels with a perforated spoon, reserving the liquid, and set aside until they are cool enough to handle. Discard any mussels that have not opened.

3 Melt the butter in a pan over a medium heat and fry the remaining onion until translucent. Stir in the garlic and cook for 1 minute. Gradually pour on the reserved cooking liquid, stirring to blend thoroughly. Stir in the parsley and cream, season and bring to simmering point. Taste and adjust the seasoning if necessary.

4 Cook the pasta in a large pan of boiling salted water, adding the oil. When it is almost tender, drain it in a colander. Return the pasta to the pan, cover and keep warm.

5 Remove the mussels from their shells, reserving a few for garnish. Stir the mussels into the cream sauce. Tip the pasta into a warmed serving dish, pour on the sauce and, using 2 large spoons, toss it well. Garnish with a few mussel shells. Serve hot, with warm, crusty bread.

PASTA SHELLS

Pasta shells, from medium-sized to giant ones, are ideal for this dish, because the rich, buttery sauce collects in the cavities and impregnates the pasta with the flavours of the shellfish and wine.

STEP 1

STEP 2

STEP 3

STEP 3

SPAGHETTI WITH SMOKED SALMON

*Made in moments, this is a dish to astonish and delight
unexpected guests.*

SERVES 4

500 g/1 lb buckwheat spaghetti
2 tbsp olive oil
90 g/3 oz/¹/₂ cup feta cheese, crumbled
salt
fresh coriander (cilantro), to garnish

SAUCE:
300 ml/¹/₂ pint/1¹/₄ cups double (heavy)
*   cream*
150 ml/¹/₄ pint/²/₃ cup whisky or brandy
125 g/4 oz smoked salmon
large pinch chilli powder
2 tbsp chopped coriander (cilantro) or fresh
*   flat-leaf parsley*
pepper

1 Cook the spaghetti in a large pan of boiling salted water, adding 1 tablespoon of the olive oil. When the pasta is almost tender, drain it in a colander. Return to the pan and sprinkle on the remaining oil. Cover and shake the pan and keep warm.

2 In separate small pans, heat the cream and the whisky or brandy to simmering point, but do not let them boil.

3 Combine the cream and whisky or brandy. Cut the smoked salmon into thin strips and add to the cream. Season with pepper and chilli powder and stir in the chopped fresh herb.

4 Transfer the spaghetti to a warmed serving dish, pour on the sauce and toss thoroughly using 2 large forks. Scatter the crumbled cheese over the pasta and garnish with coriander (cilantro) leaves. Serve at once.

ACCOMPANIMENTS

A green salad with a lemony dressing is a good accompaniment to this rich and luxurious dish.

VERMICELLI WITH CLAM SAUCE

*Another cook-in-a-hurry recipe that transforms storecupboard
ingredients into a dish with style.*

STEP 1

SERVES 4

*400 g/14 oz vermicelli, spaghetti or other
   long pasta
1 tbsp olive oil
30 g/1 oz/2 tbsp butter
2 tbsp flaked Parmesan cheese
fresh basil sprig, to garnish*

*SAUCE:
1 tbsp olive oil
2 onions, chopped
2 garlic cloves, chopped
2 × 200 g/7 oz jars clams in brine
125 ml/4 fl oz/¹/₂ cup white wine
4 tbsp chopped fresh flat-leaf parsley
¹/₂ tsp dried oregano
pinch grated nutmeg
salt and pepper*

1 Cook the pasta in a large pan of
boiling salted water, adding the
olive oil. When it is almost tender, drain
it in a colander, return to the pan and
add the butter. Cover the pan. Shake it
and keep it warm.

2 To make the clam sauce, heat the
oil in a pan over a medium heat
and fry the onion until it is translucent.
Stir in the garlic and cook for a further
minute.

3 Strain the liquid from one jar of
clams, pour into the pan and add
the wine. Stir well, bring to simmering
point and simmer for 3 minutes. Drain
the brine from the second jar of clams
and discard. Add the clams and herbs to
the pan and season with pepper and
nutmeg. Lower the heat and cook until
the sauce is heated through.

4 Transfer the pasta to a warmed
serving dish and pour on the sauce.
Sprinkle on the Parmesan and garnish
with the basil. Serve hot.

STEP 2

STEP 3

PARMESAN

You could use grated Parmesan for this
dish, but flakes of fresh Parmesan, carved
off the block, give it an added depth of
flavour.

STEP 3

STEP 2

STEP 2

STEP 3

STEP 3

SPAGHETTI WITH TUNA & PARSLEY SAUCE

This is a recipe to look forward to when parsley is at its most prolific, in the summer growing season.

SERVES 4

500 g/ 1 lb spaghetti
1 tbsp olive oil
30 g/ 1 oz/ 2 tbsp butter
black olives, to garnish

SAUCE:
200 g/ 7 oz can tuna, drained
50 g/ 2 oz can anchovies, drained
250 ml/ 8 fl oz/ 1 cup olive oil
60 g/ 2 oz/ 1 cup parsley, chopped roughly
150 ml/ ¼ pint/ ⅔ cup crème fraîche
salt and pepper

1 Cook the spaghetti in a large pan of boiling salted water, adding the olive oil. When it is almost tender, drain it in a colander and return to the pan. Add the butter, toss thoroughly to coat and keep warm.

2 Remove any bones from the tuna. Put it into a blender or food processor with the anchovies, olive oil and parsley and process until the sauce is smooth. Pour in the crème fraîche and process for a few seconds to blend. Taste the sauce and adjust the seasoning.

3 Warm 4 plates. Shake the pan of spaghetti over a medium heat until it is thoroughly warmed through, then transfer to a serving dish. Pour on the sauce and toss quickly, using 2 forks. Garnish with the olives and serve immediately with warm, crusty bread.

KNOW YOUR OIL

Oils produced by different countries, mainly Italy, Spain and Greece, have their own characteristic flavours. Some olive varieties produce an oil which has a hot and peppery taste, while others, such as the Kalamata, grown in Greece, give a distinctly 'green' flavour. Get to know and recognize the different grades of oil, too. Extra virgin olive oil, the finest grade, is made from the first, cold pressing of olives. Virgin olive oil, which has a fine aroma and colour, is also made by cold pressing, but it may have a slightly higher acidity level than extra virgin oil. Refined or pure olive oil is made by treating the paste residue with heat or solvents to remove the residual oil. Olive oil is a blend of refined and virgin olive oil.

NORTH SEA PASTA PUDDING

A tasty mixture of creamy fish and pasta cooked in a bowl, unmoulded and drizzled with tomato sauce presents macaroni in a new guise.

STEP 2

STEP 3

STEP 3

STEP 5

SERVES 4

125 g/4 oz short-cut macaroni or other
   short pasta shapes
1 tbsp olive oil
15 g/½ oz/1 tbsp butter, plus extra for
   greasing
500 g/1 lb white fish fillets, such as cod,
   haddock or coley
a few fresh parsley sprigs
6 black peppercorns
125 ml/4 oz/½ cup double (heavy) cream
2 eggs, separated
2 tbsp chopped dill or flat-leaf parsley
salt and pepper
pinch grated nutmeg
60 g/2 oz/½ cup Parmesan cheese, grated
Tomato Sauce (see page 233)
dill or flat-leaf parsley sprigs, to garnish

1 Cook the pasta in a large pan of boiling salted water, adding the oil. Drain it in a colander, return to the pan, add the butter and cover. Keep warm.

2 Place the fish in a frying pan (skillet) with the parsley and peppercorns and pour on just enough water to cover. Bring to the boil, then cover and simmer for 10 minutes. Lift out the fish with a fish slice, reserving the liquid. When the fish is cool enough to

handle, skin and remove any remaining bones. Cut into bite-sized pieces.

3 Transfer the pasta to a large bowl and stir in the cream, egg yolks, herb and pepper. Stir in the fish, taking care not to break it, and enough liquid to make a moist, firm mixture. It should fall from a spoon but not be too runny. Whisk the egg whites until stiff but not dry, then fold into the mixture.

4 Grease an ovenproof bowl or pudding basin and spoon in the mixture to within 4 cm/1½ inches of the rim. Cover with greased baking parchment and a cloth, or with foil, and tie firmly round the rim. (Do not use foil if cooking in a microwave.)

5 Stand the pudding on a trivet in a large pan of boiling water to come halfway up the sides. Cover and steam for 1½ hours, topping up the boiling water as needed, or cook in a microwave on Full Power for 7 minutes.

6 Run a knife around the inside of the bowl and invert on to a warmed platter. Pour some sauce over the top and serve the rest separately. Garnish with dill or flat-leaf parsley.

STEP 2

STEP 2

STEP 3

STEP 4

SQUID & MACARONI STEW

This Mediterranean dish is quick and easy to make, yet has all the authentic flavour of life beside the sea.

SERVES 4–6

250 g / 8 oz short-cut macaroni or other short pasta shapes
1 tbsp olive oil
2 tbsp chopped flat-leaf parsley
salt and pepper

SAUCE:
350 g / 12 oz cleaned squid (see below)
6 tbsp olive oil
2 onions, sliced
250 ml / 8 fl oz / 1 cup fish stock
150 ml / ¼ pint / ⅔ cup red wine
350 g / 12 oz tomatoes, skinned and sliced thinly
2 tbsp tomato purée (paste)
1 tsp dried oregano
2 bay leaves

1 Cook the pasta for only 3 minutes in a large pan of boiling salted water, adding the oil. When it is almost tender, drain the pasta in a colander, return to the pan, cover and keep warm.

2 Cut the squid into 4 cm / 1½ inch strips. Heat the oil in a pan over a medium heat and fry the onions until translucent. Add the squid and stock and simmer for 5 minutes. Pour on the wine and add the tomatoes, tomato purée

(paste), oregano and bay leaves. Bring the sauce to the boil, then season and cook, uncovered, for 5 minutes.

3 Add the pasta, stir well, cover the pan and continue simmering for 10 minutes or until the macaroni and squid are almost tender. By this time the sauce should be thick and syrupy. If it is too liquid, uncover the pan and continue cooking for a few minutes. Taste the sauce and adjust the seasoning if necessary.

4 Remove the bay leaves and stir in most of the parsley, reserving a little to garnish. Transfer to a warmed serving dish. Sprinkle on the remaining parsley and serve hot. Serve with warm, crusty bread such as ciabatta.

CLEANING SQUID

Peel off the skin and cut off the head and tentacles. Remove the transparent bone from the body, then turn the body sac inside out and wash thoroughly. Cut off the tentacles to use and discard the head.

CHAPTER NINE

Pasta & Vegetable Dishes

Aubergine (eggplant) shells filled with Mozzarella and pasta shapes;
crisp and crunchy vegetables like celery and
(bell) peppers stir-fried with pasta shells and tossed in a
sweet and sour sauce; a pasta omelette of just-cooked
eggs flavoured with onion, fennel and garlic – this chapter
takes you on a gastronomic tour
through Italy.

Whether you choose to simmer vegetables lightly in water or stock,
to steam them or to stir-fry them, be sure to cook them only until
they, like the pasta, are *al dente* and still slightly crisp.
In this way the vegetables will retain more of their nutrients
and most of their colour and will contrast both appealingly and
deliciously with their pasta accompaniment.

Opposite: *The rolling hills of Val d'Oreia, near Pienza, Tuscany. Much of the country's food – grains, rice, meat, fruit and vegetables – is produced in the fertile Tuscan soil.*

STEP 2

STEP 2

STEP 4

STEP 4

PASTA WITH GREEN VEGETABLES

The different shapes and textures of the vegetables make a mouthwatering presentation in this light and summery dish.

SERVES 4

250 g/8 oz gemelli or other pasta shapes
1 tbsp olive oil
2 tbsp chopped fresh flat-leaf parsley
salt and pepper

SAUCE:
1 head green broccoli, cut into florets
2 courgettes (zucchini), sliced
250 g/8 oz asparagus spears, trimmed
125 g/4 oz mangetout (snow peas),
*   trimmed*
125 g/4 oz frozen peas
30 g/1 oz/2 tbsp butter
3 tbsp vegetable stock
5 tbsp double (heavy) cream
large pinch grated nutmeg
2 tbsp grated Parmesan cheese

1 Cook the pasta in a large pan of boiling salted water, adding the olive oil. When almost tender, drain the pasta in a colander and return to the pan, cover and keep warm.

2 Steam the broccoli, courgettes (zucchini), asparagus spears and mangetout (snow peas) over a pan of boiling water until they are just beginning to soften. Remove from the heat and plunge into cold water to prevent them from cooking further in the residual heat. Drain and set them aside.

3 Cook the frozen peas in boiling salted water for 3 minutes, then drain. Refresh in cold water and drain again.

4 Put the butter and vegetable stock in a pan over a medium heat. Add all the vegetables, except the asparagus spears, and toss carefully with a wooden spoon to heat through, taking care not to break them up. Stir in the cream, allow the sauce just to heat through and season generously with salt, pepper and grated nutmeg.

5 Transfer the pasta to a warmed serving dish and stir in the chopped parsley. Spoon the sauce over and sprinkle on the Parmesan. Arrange the asparagus spears in a pattern on top. Serve hot.

STEP 1

STEP 3

STEP 5

STEP 5

BAKED PASTA & BEANS

A satisfying winter dish, this is a vegetarian version of cassoulet,
a slow-cooked, one-pot meal.

SERVES 6
OVEN: 180°C/350°F/GAS MARK 4

250 g/8 oz/generous 1 cup dried haricot
   beans, soaked and drained
250 g/8 oz penne or other short pasta
   shapes
6 tbsp olive oil
900 ml/1½ pints/3½ cups vegetable stock
2 large onions, sliced
2 garlic cloves, chopped
2 bay leaves
1 tsp dried oregano
1 tsp dried thyme
5 tbsp red wine
2 tbsp tomato purée (paste)
2 celery sticks, sliced
1 fennel bulb, sliced
125 g/4 oz mushrooms, sliced
250 g/8 oz tomatoes, sliced
1 tsp dark Muscovado sugar
4 tbsp dry white breadcrumbs
salt and pepper

1 Put the beans in a large pan, cover them with water and bring to the boil. Boil the beans rapidly for 20 minutes, then drain them.

2 Cook the pasta for only 3 minutes in a large pan of boiling salted water, adding 1 tablespoon of the oil.

When almost tender, drain the pasta in a colander and set aside.

3 Place the beans in a large flameproof casserole, pour on the vegetable stock and stir in the remaining olive oil, the onions, garlic, bay leaves, herbs, wine and tomato purée (paste).

4 Bring the stock to the boil, then cover the casserole and cook it in the preheated oven for 2 hours.

5 Add the reserved pasta, the celery, fennel, mushrooms and tomatoes, and season with salt and pepper. Stir in the sugar and sprinkle the breadcrumbs over. Cover the casserole and continue cooking it for 1 hour. Serve it hot, with salad leaves and plenty of crusty bread.

NOTE

Do not use a salted vegetable stock for the initial cooking stage of this dish, since the salt would inhibit the softening process of the beans as they gradually absorb the liquid.

STEP 2

STEP 3

STEP 4

STEP 6

VEGETABLE PASTA STIR-FRY

Prepare all the vegetables and cook the pasta in advance,
then the dish can be cooked in a few minutes.

SERVES 4

400 g/14 oz wholewheat pasta shells or
   other short pasta shapes
1 tbsp olive oil
2 carrots, sliced thinly
125 g/4 oz baby corn
3 tbsp peanut oil
2.5 cm/1 inch piece ginger root, peeled and
   sliced thinly
1 large onion, sliced thinly
1 garlic clove, sliced thinly
3 celery sticks, sliced thinly
1 small red (bell) pepper, cored, deseeded and
   sliced into julienne strips
1 small green (bell) pepper, cored, deseeded
   and sliced into matchstick strips
salt

SAUCE:
1 tsp cornflour (cornstarch)
2 tbsp water
3 tbsp soy sauce
3 tbsp dry sherry
1 tsp clear honey
few drops hot pepper sauce (optional)

1 Cook the pasta in a large pan of boiling salted water, adding the tablespoon of olive oil. When almost tender, drain the pasta in a colander, return to the pan, cover and keep warm.

2 Cook the sliced carrot and baby corn in boiling salted water for 2 minutes, then drain in a colander, plunge into cold water to prevent further cooking and drain again.

3 Heat the peanut oil in a wok or a large frying pan (skillet) over a medium heat and fry the ginger for 1 minute, to flavour the oil. Remove with a perforated spoon and discard.

4 Add the onion, garlic, celery and (bell) peppers to the oil and stir-fry for 2 minutes. Add the carrots and baby corn and stir-fry for a further 2 minutes, then stir in the reserved pasta.

5 Put the cornflour (cornstarch) into a small bowl and gradually pour on the water, stirring constantly. Stir in the soy sauce, sherry and honey.

6 Pour the sauce into the wok or frying pan (skillet), stir well and cook for 2 minutes, stirring once or twice. Taste the sauce and season with hot pepper sauce if liked. Serve with a steamed green vegetable such as mangetout (snow peas).

BAKED AUBERGINES (EGGPLANTS) WITH PASTA

Combined with tomatoes and Mozzarella, pasta makes a tasty filling for baked aubergine (eggplant) shells.

STEP 2

SERVES 4
OVEN: 200°C/400°F/GAS MARK 6

*250 g/8 oz penne or other short pasta
  shapes*
4 tbsp olive oil, plus extra for brushing
2 medium aubergines (eggplants)
1 large onion, chopped
2 garlic cloves, crushed
425 g/15 oz can chopped tomatoes
2 tsp dried oregano
60 g/2 oz Mozzarella cheese, sliced thinly
30 g/1 oz/¼ cup Parmesan cheese, grated
2 tbsp dry breadcrumbs
salt and pepper

1 Cook the pasta in a large pan of boiling salted water, adding 1 tablespoon of the olive oil. When it is almost tender, drain the pasta in a colander, return to the pan, cover and keep warm.

2 Cut the aubergines (eggplants) in half lengthways. Score around the inside with a knife, then scoop out the flesh with a spoon, taking care not to pierce the skin. Brush the insides of the aubergine (eggplant) shells with olive oil. Chop the aubergine (eggplant) flesh and set it aside.

3 Heat the remaining oil in a frying pan (skillet) over a medium heat and fry the onion until it is translucent. Add the garlic and fry for 1 minute. Add the chopped aubergine (eggplant) and fry for 5 minutes, stirring frequently. Add the tomatoes and oregano and season with salt and pepper. Bring to the boil and simmer for 10 minutes or until the mixture is thick. Taste and adjust the seasoning if necessary. Remove from the heat and stir in the reserved pasta.

4 Brush a baking sheet (cookie sheet) with oil and arrange the aubergine (eggplant) shells in a single layer. Divide half the tomato mixture between the 4 shells. Arrange the Mozzarella on top and cover with the remaining mixture, piling it into a mound. Mix together the Parmesan and breadcrumbs, then sprinkle over the top, patting it lightly into the mixture.

5 Bake in a preheated oven for 25 minutes until the topping is golden brown. Serve hot, with a green salad.

STEP 3

STEP 4

STEP 4

STEP 2

STEP 3

STEP 3

STEP 5

VERMICELLI FLAN

Lightly cooked vermicelli is pressed into a flan ring and baked with a creamy mushroom filling.

SERVES 4
OVEN: 180°C / 350°F / GAS MARK 4

250 g/8 oz vermicelli or spaghetti
1 tbsp olive oil
30 g/1 oz/2 tbsp butter, plus extra for
  greasing
salt

SAUCE:
60 g/2 oz/¼ cup butter
1 onion, chopped
150 g/5 oz button mushrooms, trimmed
1 green (bell) pepper, cored, deseeded and
  sliced into thin rings
150 ml/¼ pint/⅔ cup milk
3 eggs, lightly beaten
2 tbsp double (heavy) cream
1 tsp dried oregano
pinch grated nutmeg
pepper
1 tbsp grated Parmesan cheese

1 Cook the pasta in a large pan of boiling salted water, adding olive oil. When almost tender, drain it in a colander. Return to the pan, add the butter and shake the pan.

2 Grease a 20 cm/8 inch loose-bottom flan tin (pan). Press the pasta on the base and round the sides to form a case.

3 Heat the butter in a frying pan (skillet) over a medium heat and fry the onion well until it is translucent. Remove with a perforated spoon and spread it in the flan base.

4 Add the mushrooms and (bell) pepper rings to the pan and turn them in the fat until they are glazed. Fry them for about 2 minutes on each side, then arrange in the flan case.

5 Beat together the milk, eggs and cream, stir in the oregano and season with nutmeg and pepper. Pour the custard mixture carefully over the vegetables and sprinkle on the cheese.

6 Bake the flan in the preheated oven for 40–45 minutes, until the filling is set. Slide on to a serving plate and serve warm.

VARIATIONS

You can use this moist and buttery flan case with any of your favourite fillings: chopped bacon, cheese and herbs, or a mixture of diced ham and sliced mushrooms; or cooked and flaked smoked haddock with sweetcorn kernels.

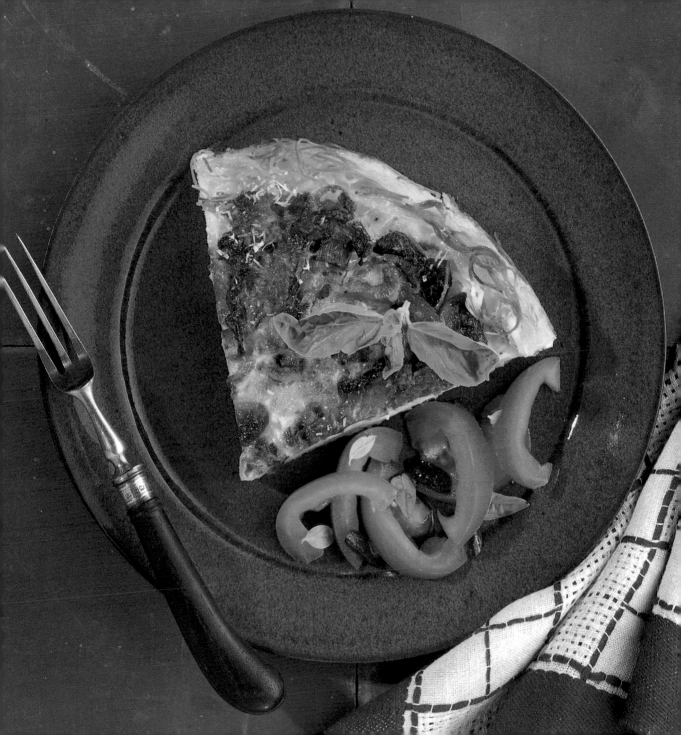

PASTA OMELETTE

Use any leftover cooked pasta you may have, such as penne, short-cut macaroni or shells, to make this fluffy omelette an instant success.

STEP 3

STEP 3

STEP 3

STEP 4

SERVES 2

4 tbsp olive oil
1 small Spanish onion, chopped
1 fennel bulb, sliced thinly
125 g/4 oz raw potato, diced and dried
1 garlic clove, chopped
4 eggs
1 tbsp chopped fresh flat-leaf parsley
pinch chilli powder
90 g/3 oz short pasta, cooked weight
1 tbsp stuffed green olives, halved, plus extra
   to garnish
salt and pepper
fresh marjoram sprigs, to garnish

1 Heat 2 tablespoons of the oil in a heavy frying pan (skillet) over a low heat and fry the onion, fennel and potato for 8–10 minutes, stirring occasionally, until the potato is just tender. Do not allow it to break up. Stir in the garlic and cook for 1 further minute. Remove the pan from the heat, lift out the vegetables with a perforated spoon and set aside. Rinse and dry the pan.

2 Break the eggs into a bowl and beat them until they are frothy. Stir in the parsley and season with salt, pepper and chilli powder.

3 Heat 1 tablespoon of the remaining oil in a pan over a medium heat. Pour in half the beaten eggs, then add the cooked vegetables, the pasta and the olives. Pour on the remaining egg and cook until the sides begin to set.

4 Lift up the edges with a palette knife (spatula) to allow the uncooked egg to spread underneath. Continue cooking the omelette, shaking the pan occasionally, until the underside is golden brown.

5 Slide the omelette out on to a large, flat plate and wipe the pan clean with paper towels. Heat the remaining oil in the pan and invert the omelette. Cook on the other side until it is also golden brown.

6 Slide the omelette on to a warmed serving dish. Garnish with a few olives and fresh marjoram, and serve hot, cut into wedges, with a tomato salad.

150

3
PIZZAS

CHAPTER TEN

Basics

The success of a pizza depends on the quality of the bread dough base and the tomato sauce. A homemade bread dough base topped with a delicious freshly made tomato sauce will give you the closest thing possible to an authentic Italian pizza in your own kitchen. If time is short and you cannot wait for the dough to rise, make either a scone (biscuit) or a potato base. Alternatively, ready-made bases or pizza-base mixes can suffice, but these do not provide the same aroma of home-baked bread, nor the sense of achievement.

Choose tomatoes that are canned in juice rather than water, as these make a thicker sauce. Many brands of chopped tomatoes have added ingredients such as garlic, chilli, onion, basil and mixed herbs, which will add extra flavour to your tomato sauces. For pizza fans and busy cooks, make double the quantity of the basic bread dough and freeze the dough that is not required after it has been kneaded. Or you can roll out the dough in the usual way, arrange the topping on it and bake for 10 minutes, then cool and freeze. Reheat by cooking from frozen for 15 minutes. The tomato sauces also freeze well, so make up large quantities and freeze the excess, and then you can have pizzas whenever you wish.

Opposite: The many-levelled red tile roofs and deep green trees of a typical Italian hill town.

BREAD DOUGH BASE

Traditionally, pizza bases are made from bread dough; this recipe will give you a base similar to an Italian pizza. Always use plain (all-purpose) flour which can be white, wholemeal (whole wheat) or a combination of both.

STEP 3

STEP 4

STEP 5

STEP 6

MAKES ONE 25 CM/10 INCH ROUND

*15 g/¹/₂ oz fresh (compressed) yeast or 1 tsp
    dried or easy-blend yeast*
90 ml/ 3¹/₂ fl oz/ 7 tbsp tepid water
¹/₂ tsp sugar
1 tbsp olive oil
*175 g/6 oz/ 1¹/₂ cups plain (all-purpose)
    flour*
1 tsp salt

1 Combine the fresh yeast with the water and sugar in a bowl. If using dried yeast, sprinkle it over the surface of the water and whisk in until dissolved.

2 Leave the mixture to rest in a warm place for 10–15 minutes until frothy on the surface. Stir in the olive oil.

3 Sift the flour and salt into a large bowl. If using easy-blend yeast, stir it in at this point. Make a well in the centre and pour in the yeast liquid, or water and oil (without the sugar for easy-blend yeast).

4 Using floured hands or a wooden spoon, mix together to form a dough. Turn out on to a floured work surface (counter) and knead for about 5

minutes until smooth and elastic.

5 Place in a large greased plastic bag and leave in a warm place for about 1 hour or until doubled in size. (Airing cupboards are good places for this, as the temperature remains constant.)

6 Turn out on to a lightly floured work surface (counter) and knock back (punch down) by punching the dough. This releases any air bubbles which would make the pizza uneven. Knead 4 or 5 times. The dough is now ready to use.

FREEZING

Pizza dough can be frozen after the first kneading. Wrap in clingfilm (plastic wrap) and label with the date and quantity before freezing. Defrost at room temperature and leave to rise in the usual way. Continue as from step 5.

STEP 2

STEP 3

STEP 4

STEP 5

SCONE (BISCUIT) BASE

This is a quick and easy alternative to the bread dough base. If you do not have time to wait for bread dough to rise, a scone (biscuit) base is the next best thing.

MAKES ONE 25 CM/10 INCH ROUND

175 g/6 oz/1½ cups self-raising flour
½ tsp salt
30 g/1 oz/2 tbsp butter, diced
120 ml/4 fl oz/½ cup milk

1 Sift the flour and salt into a large mixing bowl.

2 Rub in the butter with your fingertips until the mixture resembles fine breadcrumbs.

3 Make a well in the centre of the flour and butter mixture and pour in nearly all the milk at once. Mix in quickly with a knife. Add the remaining milk only if needed to make a soft dough.

4 Turn the dough out on to a floured work surface (counter) and knead by turning and pressing with the heel of your hand 3 or 4 times.

5 Either roll out or press the dough into a 25 cm/10 inch circle on a lightly greased baking sheet (cookie sheet) or pizza pan. Push up the edge all round slightly to form a ridge and use immediately.

ADDING TASTE

You can vary the taste of your scone (biscuit) base by adding a little grated cheese or ½ teaspoon dried oregano or mixed herbs to it for a more interesting flavour. Add your extra flavourings to the mixture after rubbing in the butter.

RUBBING IN

When rubbing in butter, it helps if your hands and the butter are very cold. Cut the butter into small dice first, then cut it into the flour with 2 knives held like scissors. Finally, rub in the remaining lumps of butter with your fingertips, remembering to keep your hands cool as you go.

STEP 1

STEP 2

STEP 3

STEP 4

POTATO BASE

This is an unusual pizza base made from mashed potatoes and flour and is a great way to use up any leftover boiled potatoes. Children love this base and you will soon have them asking for more.

MAKES ONE 25 CM/10 INCH ROUND

250 g/8 oz boiled potatoes
60 g/2 oz/4 tbsp butter or margarine
125 g/4 oz/1 cup self-raising flour
¹/₂ tsp salt

1 If the potatoes are hot, mash them, then stir in the butter until it has melted and is distributed evenly throughout the potatoes. Leave to cool.

2 Sift the flour and salt together, stir into the mashed potato mixture and mix together to form a soft dough.

3 If the potatoes are cold, mash them without adding the butter. Sift the flour and salt into a bowl. Rub in the butter with your fingertips until the mixture resembles fine breadcrumbs, then stir the flour and butter mixture into the mashed potatoes to form a soft dough.

4 Either roll out or press the dough into a 25 cm/10 inch circle on a lightly greased baking sheet (cooking sheet) or pizza pan, pushing up the edge all round slightly to form a ridge before adding the topping. This base is tricky to lift before it is cooked, so you will find it easier to handle if you roll it out directly on the baking sheet (cooking sheet).

5 If the base is not required for cooking immediately, you can cover it with clingfilm (plastic wrap) and chill it for up to 2 hours.

USING INSTANT COOKED POTATOES

If time is short and you do not have any leftover cooked potatoes, make up a batch of instant dried mashed potato, keeping the consistency fairly dry, and use that instead – it will work just as well.

EXTRA FLAVOUR

To add more flavour to this base, you can include dried or fresh herbs, fried chopped onion, grated cheese or even a grated carrot. Any of these will add a delicious subtle taste to your pizza base.

TOMATO SAUCE

Use cans of either chopped or whole plum tomatoes for this sauce. Many cooks prefer to use chopped tomatoes as it saves time, and the plum tomatoes tend to be on the watery side. For a really spicy sauce, add a chopped fresh red chilli when frying the onions.

STEP 1

MAKES ENOUGH TO COVER ONE
25 CM/10 INCH PIZZA BASE

1 small onion, chopped
1 garlic clove, crushed
1 tbsp olive oil
220 g/7 oz can chopped tomatoes
2 tsp tomato purée (paste)
$^{1}/_{2}$ tsp sugar
$^{1}/_{2}$ tsp dried oregano
1 bay leaf
salt and pepper

1 Fry the onion and garlic gently in the oil for 5 minutes until softened but not browned.

2 Add the tomatoes, tomato purée (paste), sugar, oregano, bay leaf and seasoning. Stir well.

3 Bring to the boil, then cover and simmer gently for 20 minutes, stirring occasionally, until you have a thickish sauce.

4 Remove the bay leaf and adjust the seasoning to taste. Leave to cool completely before using. This sauce keeps well in a screw-top jar in the refrigerator for up to 1 week.

TOMATOES

Tomatoes are actually berries and are related to potatoes. There are many different shapes and sizes of this versatile fruit. The one most used in Italian cooking is the plum tomato. Large beefsteak tomatoes or small, sweet cherry tomatoes are ideal for use in accompanying salads.

USING CHILLIES

Take care when chopping chillies as they can burn your skin. Handle them as little as possible – you can even wear rubber gloves if you wish. Always wash your hands thoroughly afterwards, and don't touch your face or eyes before you have washed your hands.

Remove chilli seeds before chopping the chillies, as they are the hottest part, and shouldn't be allowed to slip into the food.

STEP 2

STEP 3

STEP 4

STEP 1

STEP 2

STEP 3

STEP 4

SPECIAL TOMATO SAUCE

This sauce is made with fresh tomatoes. Use the plum variety whenever available and always choose the reddest tomatoes to give a better colour and sweetness to the sauce. When fresh plum tomatoes are readily available, make several batches of sauce and freeze them.

MAKES ENOUGH TO COVER ONE
25 CM/10 INCH PIZZA BASE

1 small onion, chopped
1 small red (bell) pepper, cored, deseeded and
   chopped
1 garlic clove, crushed
2 tbsp olive oil
250 g/8 oz tomatoes
1 tbsp tomato purée (paste)
1 tsp soft brown sugar
2 tsp chopped fresh basil
$^1/_2$ tsp dried oregano
1 bay leaf
salt and pepper

1 Fry the onion, (bell) pepper and garlic gently in the oil for 5 minutes until softened but not browned.

2 Cut a cross in the base of each tomato and place them in a bowl. Pour on boiling water and leave for about 45 seconds. Drain, and then plunge in cold water. The skins will slide off easily.

3 Chop the tomatoes, discarding any hard cores. Add the chopped tomatoes, tomato purée (paste), sugar, herbs and seasoning to the onion mixture. Stir well. Bring to the boil, then cover and simmer gently for 30 minutes, stirring occasionally, until you have a thickish sauce.

4 Remove the bay leaf and adjust the seasoning to taste. Leave to cool completely before using.

5 This sauce will keep well in a screw-top jar in the refrigerator for up to 1 week.

SKINNING TOMATOES

You can skin tomatoes in another way if you have a gas stove. Cut a cross in the base of the tomato, push it on to a fork and hold it over a gas flame, turning it slowly so that the skin heats evenly all over. The skin will start to bubble and split, and should then slide off easily.

CHAPTER ELEVEN

Meat & Fish Pizzas

A meat or fish pizza provides a very substantial, well-balanced meal. Pizzas can be topped with almost any type of meat or fish, which can lead to many highly imaginative dishes.
As pizzas are baked in a hot oven for a fairly short time, the meat should be cooked before it is added to the pizza, or it will end up undercooked. For the best results the meat should be minced (ground) or cut into small pieces. Bacon can be added in its raw state as this is usually thinly sliced and cooks very quickly. There are almost endless varieties of salamis, sliced cured meats, hams, sausages and bacon, either pre-packaged or from the delicatessen counter, which make perfect pizza toppings.

Canned or fresh fish or shellfish are wonderful on pizzas. Use anything from whole fresh whitebait, mussels or clams in their shells, canned sardines and monkfish to just plain cod. The most popular fish known to the pizza are, of course, anchovies and you either love them or hate them. One of the most famous pizzas on which they are used is the Pizza Napoletana, which is found in Naples; the topping is basically anchovies and olives without any cheese. If you find anchovies too salty, it helps to soak them in a little milk before using.

Opposite: *Sunset over the Grand Canal, Venice.*

STEP 1

STEP 3

STEP 4

STEP 6

CHICKEN SATAY

Chicken satay is usually served with a peanut sauce, so this pizza is topped with chicken which has been marinated in a peanut sauce. For an even simpler version, just use the crunchy peanut butter.

SERVES 2–4
OVEN: 200°C/400°F/GAS MARK 6

2 tbsp crunchy peanut butter
1 tbsp lime juice
1 tbsp soy sauce
3 tbsp milk
1 red chilli, deseeded and chopped
1 garlic clove, crushed
175 g/6 oz cooked chicken, diced
1 quantity Bread Dough Base (see
    page 156)
1 quantity Special Tomato Sauce (see
    page 164)
4 spring onions (scallions), trimmed and
    chopped
60 g/2 oz Mozzarella cheese, grated
olive oil for drizzling
salt and pepper

1 Mix together the peanut butter, lime juice, soy sauce, milk, chilli and garlic in a bowl to form a sauce. Season well.

2 Add the chicken to the peanut sauce and stir until well coated. Cover and leave to marinate in a cool place for about 20 minutes.

3 Roll out or press the dough, using a rolling pin or your hands, into a 25 cm/10 inch circle on a lightly floured work surface (counter). Place on a large greased baking sheet (cookie sheet) or pizza pan and push up the edge a little. Cover and leave to rise slightly for 10 minutes in a warm place.

4 When the dough has risen, spread with the tomato sauce almost to the edge.

5 Top with the spring onions (scallions) and chicken pieces, spooning over the peanut sauce.

6 Sprinkle over the cheese. Drizzle with a little olive oil and season well. Bake in a preheated oven for 18–20 minutes or until the crust is golden. Serve immediately.

TIMESAVERS

If you are short of time, buy ready-cooked chicken, remove any skin and cut it into chunks. You can save even more time by using crunchy peanut butter instead of making the satay sauce.

HOT CHILLI BEEF

This deep-pan pizza is topped with minced (ground) beef, red kidney beans and jalapeño chillies, which are small, green and hot. Add more or less chilli powder depending on taste. Monterey Jack is an American cheese; if it is unavailable, use a mature (sharp) Cheddar instead.

SERVES 2–4
OVEN: 220°C/400°F/GAS MARK 6

FOR THE DOUGH BASE:
20 g/³/₄ oz fresh (compressed) yeast or
  1¹/₂ tsp dried or easy-blend yeast
125 ml/4 fl oz/¹/₂ cup tepid water
1 tsp sugar
3 tbsp olive oil
250 g/8 oz/2 cups plain (all-purpose) flour
1 tsp salt

FOR THE TOPPING:
1 small onion, sliced thinly
1 garlic clove, crushed
¹/₂ yellow (bell) pepper, cored, deseeded and
  chopped
1 tbsp olive oil
175 g/6 oz lean minced (ground) beef
¹/₄ tsp chilli powder
¹/₄ tsp ground cumin
220 g/7 oz can red kidney beans, drained
1 quantity Tomato Sauce (see page 163)
30 g/1 oz jalapeño chillies, sliced
60 g/2 oz Mozzarella cheese, sliced thinly
60 g/2 oz Monterey Jack cheese, grated
olive oil for drizzling
salt and pepper
chopped fresh flat-leaf parsley, to garnish

1 To make the deep-pan dough base, use the same method as for

making the Bread Dough Base recipe (see page 156).

2 Roll out or press the dough, using a rolling pin or your hands, into a 23 cm/9 inch circle on a lightly floured work surface (counter). Place on a pizza pan and push up the edge to fit and form a small ridge. Cover and leave to rise slightly for about 10 minutes.

3 Fry the onion, garlic and (bell) pepper gently in the oil for 5 minutes until softened but not browned. Increase the heat slightly and add the beef, chilli and cumin. Fry for 5 minutes, stirring occasionally. Remove from the heat, stir in the kidney beans and season.

4 Spread the tomato sauce over the dough almost to the edge and top with the meat mixture.

5 Top with the sliced chillies and Mozzarella and sprinkle over the grated cheese. Drizzle with a little olive oil and season.

6 Bake in a preheated oven for 18–20 minutes or until the crust is golden. Serve immediately sprinkled with chopped parsley.

STEP 2

STEP 3

STEP 4

STEP 5

AUBERGINE (EGGPLANT) & LAMB

An unusual fragrant, spiced pizza topped with minced (ground) lamb
and aubergine (eggplant) on a bread base. Pimientos are skinned, sweet,
elongated red (bell) peppers, which are available canned in oil or brine;
if these are unavailable, use sliced red (bell) pepper instead.

STEP 1

SERVES 2–4
OVEN: 200°C/400°F/GAS MARK 6

1 small aubergine (eggplant), diced
1 quantity Bread Dough Base (see
   page 156)
1 tsp cumin seeds
1 tbsp olive oil
175 g/6 oz minced (ground) lamb
30 g/1 oz pimiento, sliced thinly
2 tbsp chopped fresh coriander (cilantro)
1 quantity Special Tomato Sauce (see
   page 164)
90 g/3 oz Mozzarella cheese, sliced thinly
olive oil for drizzling
salt and pepper

1 Sprinkle the diced aubergine
(eggplant) with salt in a colander
and let the bitter juices drain over a sink
for about 20 minutes; then rinse and pat
dry with paper towels.

2 Roll out or press the dough, using
a rolling pin or your hands, into a
25 cm/10 inch circle on a lightly floured
work surface (counter). Place on a large
greased baking sheet (cookie sheet) or
pizza pan and push up the edge a little to
form a rim.

STEP 2

3 Cover and leave to rise slightly for
10 minutes in a warm place.

4 Fry the onion, garlic and cumin
seeds gently in the oil for 3
minutes. Increase the heat slightly and
add the lamb, aubergine (eggplant) and
pimiento. Fry for 5 minutes, stirring
occasionally. Add the coriander
(cilantro) and season well.

5 Spread the tomato sauce over the
dough base almost to the edge. Top
with the lamb mixture.

6 Arrange the Mozzarella slices on
top. Drizzle over a little olive oil and
season to taste.

7 Bake in a preheated oven for
18–20 minutes, until the crust is
crisp and golden. Serve immediately.

STEP 4

CORIANDER (CILANTRO)

If fresh coriander (cilantro) is unavailable,
substitute 1 tsp ground coriander and add
1 tbsp chopped fresh parsley for colour.

STEP 6

STEP 1

STEP 2

STEP 3

STEP 4

SMOKY BACON & PEPPERONI

This more traditional kind of pizza is topped with pepperoni, smoked bacon and (bell) peppers covered with a smoked cheese.

SERVES 2–4
OVEN: 200°C/400°F/GAS MARK 6

*1 quantity Bread Dough Base (see
 page 156)
1 tbsp olive oil
1 tbsp grated Parmesan cheese
1 quantity Tomato Sauce (see page 163)
125 g/4 oz lightly smoked bacon, diced
1/2 green (bell) pepper, cored, deseeded and
 sliced thinly
1/2 yellow (bell) pepper, cored, deseeded and
 sliced thinly
60 g/2 oz pepperoni-style sliced spicy
 sausage
60 g/2 oz smoked Bavarian cheese, grated
1/2 tsp dried oregano
olive oil for drizzling
salt and pepper*

1 Roll out or press the dough, using a rolling pin or your hands, into a 25 cm/10 inch circle on a lightly floured work surface (counter). Place on a large greased baking sheet (cookie sheet) or pizza pan and push up the edge a little with your fingers to form a rim.

2 Brush the base with the olive oil and sprinkle the Parmesan over it. Cover and leave to rise slightly in a warm place for about 10 minutes.

3 Spread the tomato sauce over the base almost to the edge. Top with the bacon and (bell) peppers. Arrange the pepperoni slices over and sprinkle with the smoked cheese.

4 Sprinkle over the oregano and drizzle with a little olive oil. Season well.

5 Bake in a preheated oven for 18–20 minutes or until the crust is golden and crisp around the edge. Cut into wedges and serve immediately.

SAVING TIME

Pre-packaged, thinly sliced pepperoni and diced bacon can be purchased from most supermarkets, which helps to save on preparation time.

PEPPERONI

A spicy pepperoni-style sausage can be quite hot. If you prefer a milder taste, use slices of salami, chorizo or even sliced, cooked sausages in its place.

STEP 1

STEP 3

STEP 3

STEP 4

FOUR SEASONS

This is a traditional pizza on which the toppings are divided into four sections, each of which is supposed to depict a season of the year. Sliced pepperoni, salami or kabanos (a small, spicy sausage) can be used instead of the chorizo.

SERVES 2–4
OVEN: 200°C/400°F/GAS MARK 6

1 quantity Bread Dough Base (see
   page 156)
1 quantity Special Tomato Sauce (see
   page 164)
30 g/1 oz chorizo sausage, sliced thinly
30 g/1 oz button mushrooms, wiped and
   sliced thinly
45g/1¹/₂ oz artichoke hearts, sliced thinly
30 g/1 oz Mozzarella cheese, sliced thinly
3 anchovies, halved lengthways
2 tsp capers
4 pitted black olives, sliced
4 fresh basil leaves, shredded
olive oil for drizzling
salt and pepper

1 Roll out or press the dough, using a rolling pin or your hands, into a 25 cm/10 inch circle on a lightly floured work surface (counter). Place on a large greased baking sheet (cookie sheet) or pizza pan and push up the edge a little.

2 Cover and leave to rise slightly for 10 minutes in a warm place before spreading with tomato sauce almost to the edge.

3 Put the sliced chorizo on a quarter of the pizza, the sliced mushrooms on another, the artichoke hearts on a third and the Mozzarella and anchovies on the fourth.

4 Dot the pizza with the capers, olives and basil leaves. Drizzle a little olive oil over the pizza and season. Do not put any salt on the anchovy section as the fish are very salty.

5 Bake in a preheated oven for 18–20 minutes or until the crust is golden and crisp. Serve immediately.

FISHY ALTERNATIVE

Fish-lovers could make a seafood four seasons pizza using prawns (shrimp), cockles, mussels and anchovies with one ingredient on each quarter, placed in a decorative arrangement.

STEP 1

STEP 2

STEP 3

STEP 4

MARINARA

This pizza is topped with frozen mixed seafood such as prawns (shrimp), mussels, cockles and squid rings. Alternatively, fresh seafood can be bought from the fresh fish counter in most supermarkets. If you prefer, you can just use peeled prawns (shrimp).

SERVES 2–4
OVEN: 200°C/400°F/GAS MARK 6

1 quantity Potato Base (see page 160)
1 quantity Special Tomato Sauce (see
   page 164)
200 g/7 oz frozen seafood cocktail, defrosted
1 tbsp capers
1 small yellow (bell) pepper, cored, deseeded
   and chopped
1 tbsp chopped fresh marjoram
1/2 tsp dried oregano
60 g/2 oz Mozzarella cheese, grated
1 tbsp grated Parmesan cheese
12 black olives
olive oil for drizzling
salt and pepper
sprig of fresh marjoram or oregano, to
   garnish

1 Roll out or press out the potato dough, using a rolling pin or your hands, into a 25 cm/10 inch circle on a lightly floured work surface (counter). Place on a large greased baking sheet (cookie sheet) or pizza pan and push up the edge a little with your fingers to form a rim.

2 Spread with the tomato sauce almost to the edge.

3 Arrange the seafood cocktail, capers and yellow (bell) pepper on the sauce.

4 Sprinkle over the herbs and cheeses. Arrange the olives on top. Drizzle over a little olive oil and season well with salt and pepper.

5 Bake in a preheated oven for 18–20 minutes until the edge of the pizza is crisp and golden.

6 Transfer to a warmed serving plate, garnish with a sprig of marjoram or oregano and serve immediately.

SEAFOOD TOPPING

If you prefer, you can replace any of the seafood with small pieces of monkfish, plaice, cod or slices of crabstick.

STEP 1

STEP 3

STEP 4

STEP 5

SALMON PIZZA

Chunks of canned salmon top this tasty pizza. You can use either red or pink salmon. Red salmon will give a better colour and flavour but it can be expensive.

SERVES 2–4
OVEN: 200°C/400°F/GAS MARK 6

1 quantity Scone (Biscuit) Base (see page 158)
1 quantity Tomato Sauce (see page 163)
1 courgette (zucchini), grated
1 tomato, sliced thinly
100 g/3½ oz can red or pink salmon
60 g/2 oz button mushrooms, wiped and sliced
1 tbsp chopped fresh dill
½ tsp dried oregano
45 g/1½ oz Mozzarella cheese, grated
olive oil for drizzling
salt and pepper
sprig of fresh dill, to garnish

1 Roll out or press the dough, using a rolling pin or your hands, into a 25 cm/10 inch circle on a lightly floured work surface (counter). Place on a large greased baking sheet (cookie sheet) or pizza pan and push up the edge a little with your fingers to form a rim.

2 Spread with the tomato sauce almost to the edge.

3 Top the tomato sauce with the grated courgette (zucchini), then lay the tomato slices on top.

4 Drain the can of salmon. Remove any bones and skin and flake the fish. Arrange on the pizza with the mushrooms. Sprinkle over the herbs and cheese. Drizzle with a little olive oil and season well.

5 Bake in a preheated oven for 18–20 minutes or until the edge is golden and crisp.

6 Transfer to a warmed serving plate and serve immediately, garnished with a sprig of dill.

ECONOMY VERSION

If salmon is too pricy, use either canned tuna or sardines to make a delicious everyday fish pizza. Choose canned fish in brine for a healthier topping. If fresh dill is unavailable, you can use parsley instead.

CHAPTER TWELVE

Vegetarian Pizzas

Although this chapter is for vegetarians, anyone can enjoy these pizzas. With a little imagination there is no end to the variety of vegetarian pizzas that can be produced, and as vegetables are so full of colour, they make attractive and tempting toppings. Choose the best quality fresh vegetables and herbs to give maximum flavour. Tofu and quorn make very good pizza toppings and they marinate particularly well. For extra flavour use a smoked tofu. Minced (ground) quorn (a myco-protein derived from fungus) can be used in place of minced (ground) meat in any pizza to make a vegetarian version.

A wide variety of antipasti are sold in jars of olive oil, such as artichoke hearts, sun-dried tomatoes, sliced (bell) peppers and mushrooms, which make perfect pizza topping ingredients. Use the oil in the jar to drizzle over the pizza before baking to keep it moist. If you prefer, you can use vegetarian Cheddar or Mozzarella, which are widely available. You can substitute the vegetarian variety for the cheese suggested in most of the recipes in this section (except in the Three Cheese and Artichoke recipe on page 189) for a slightly different taste.

Opposite: *The sun sets over the lush Chianti vineyards in Tuscany.*

STEP 1

STEP 3

STEP 4

STEP 5

FLORENTINE

A pizza adaptation of Eggs Florentine – sliced hard-boiled (hard-cooked) eggs on freshly cooked spinach with a little nutmeg. The breadcrumbs and almonds give the pizza topping an extra crunch.

SERVES 2–4
OVEN: 200°C/400°F/GAS MARK 6

2 tbsp grated Parmesan cheese
1 quantity Potato Base (see page 160)
1 quantity Tomato Sauce (see page 163)
175 g/6 oz fresh spinach leaves
1 small red onion, sliced thinly
2 tbsp olive oil
1/4 tsp freshly grated nutmeg
2 hard-boiled (hard-cooked) eggs
15 g/1/2 oz/1/4 cup fresh white breadcrumbs
60 g/2 oz Jarlsberg cheese, grated (or
   Emmental, Cheddar or Gruyère, if not
   available)
2 tbsp flaked (slivered) almonds
olive oil for drizzling
salt and pepper

1 Mix the Parmesan with the potato base. Roll out or press the dough, using a rolling pin or your hands, into a 25 cm/10 inch circle on a lightly floured work surface (counter). Place on a large greased baking sheet (cookie sheet) or pizza pan and push up the edge slightly. Spread with the tomato sauce almost to the edge.

2 Remove the spinach stalks (stems) and wash the leaves in plenty of cold water. Drain the spinach well and

pat off the excess water with paper towels.

3 Fry the onion gently in the oil for 5 minutes until softened. Add the spinach and continue to fry until just wilted. Drain off any excess liquid produced. Place on the pizza and sprinkle over the nutmeg.

4 Remove the shells from the eggs and slice. Arrange on the spinach.

5 Mix together the breadcrumbs, cheese and almonds, and sprinkle over. Drizzle with a little olive oil and season well.

6 Bake in a preheated oven for 18–20 minutes or until the edge is crisp and golden. Serve immediately.

SPINACH

If fresh spinach is unavailable, use frozen whole leaf spinach. Spinach carries a lot of water so drain out as much as possible or you will end up with a soggy base.

STEP 1

STEP 2

STEP 3

STEP 6

RATATOUILLE & LENTIL

The ultimate vegetarian pizza! Ratatouille and lentils on a wholemeal (whole wheat) bread base are topped with vegetarian Cheddar and sunflower seeds. You can use canned green lentils, which do not have to be soaked or cooked before being used; you will need about 125 g/4 oz.

SERVES 2–4
OVEN: 200°C/400°F/GAS MARK 6

60 g/2 oz green lentils
$1/2$ small aubergine (eggplant), diced
1 small onion, sliced
1 garlic clove, crushed
3 tbsp olive oil
$1/2$ courgette (zucchini), sliced
$1/2$ red (bell) pepper, sliced
$1/2$ green (bell) pepper, sliced
220 g/$7^1/_2$ oz can chopped tomatoes
1 tbsp chopped fresh oregano or 1 tsp dried
1 quantity Bread Dough Base made with
    wholemeal (whole wheat) flour (see
    page 156)
60 g/2 oz vegetarian Cheddar cheese,
    sliced thinly
1 tbsp sunflower seeds
olive oil for drizzling
salt and pepper

1 Soak the lentils in hot water for 30 minutes. Drain and rinse; then simmer in a pan covered with fresh water for 10 minutes.

2 Sprinkle the aubergine (eggplant) with a little salt in a colander and allow the bitter juices to drain over a sink for about 20 minutes. Rinse and pat dry with paper towels.

3 Fry the onion and garlic gently in the oil for 3 minutes. Add the courgette (zucchini), (bell) peppers and aubergine (eggplant). Cover and leave to 'sweat' over a low heat for about 5 minutes.

4 Add the tomatoes, drained lentils, oregano, 2 tablespoons water and seasoning. Cover and simmer for 15 minutes, stirring occasionally, adding more water if necessary.

5 Roll out or press the dough, using a rolling pin or your hands, into a 25 cm/10 inch circle on a lightly floured work surface (counter). Place on a large greased baking sheet (cookie sheet) or pizza pan and push up the edge slightly. Cover and leave to rise slightly for 10 minutes in a warm place.

6 Spread the ratatouille over the dough base almost to the edge. Arrange the cheese slices on top and sprinkle over the sunflower seeds. Drizzle with a little olive oil and season.

7 Bake in a preheated oven for 18–20 minutes or until the edge is crisp and golden. Serve immediately.

THREE CHEESE & ARTICHOKE

Sliced artichokes combined with Dolcelatte, Cheddar and Parmesan cheeses give a really delicious topping to this pizza. Artichoke hearts can be bought either canned or in jars in olive oil. If you use the ones in oil, you can use the oil to drizzle over the pizza before baking.

STEP 1

SERVES 2–4
OVEN: 200°C/400°F/GAS MARK 6

1 quantity Bread Dough Base (see page 156)
1 quantity Special Tomato Sauce (see page 164)
60 g/2 oz Dolcelatte cheese, sliced
125 g/4 oz artichoke hearts in oil, sliced
½ small red onion, chopped
45 g/1½ oz Cheddar cheese, grated
2 tbsp grated Parmesan cheese
1 tbsp chopped fresh thyme
oil from artichokes for drizzling
salt and pepper

1 Roll out or press the dough, using a rolling pin or your hands, into a 25 cm/10 inch circle on a lightly floured work surface (counter). Place the base on a large greased baking sheet (cookie sheet) or pizza pan and push up the edge slightly.

2 Cover and leave to rise for 10 minutes in a warm place. Spread with the tomato sauce almost to the edge.

3 Arrange the Dolcelatte on the tomato sauce, followed by the artichoke hearts and red onion.

4 Mix the Cheddar and Parmesan together with the thyme and sprinkle the mixture over the pizza. Drizzle a little of the oil from the jar of artichokes over the pizza and season to taste.

5 Bake in a preheated oven for 18–20 minutes or until the edge is crisp and golden and the cheese is bubbling.

6 Serve immediately with a fresh salad of lettuce leaves and cherry tomato halves.

STEP 3

STEP 4

STEP 6

CHEESES AND SALADS

You can use any cheese of your choice, as long as it complements the others. Remember that a strongly flavoured cheese will dominate the others. For the accompanying salad, buy a bag of mixed prepared lettuce leaves, as it saves buying several whole lettuces of different kinds.

STEP 1

STEP 2

STEP 3

STEP 4

GIARDINIERA

As the name implies, this colourful pizza should be topped with fresh vegetables grown in the garden, but as many of us do not have space to grow anything more than a few flowers, we have to rely on other sources. The vegetables used here are only a suggestion; you can replace them with the same quantity of anything that is available.

SERVES 2–4
OVEN: 200°C/400°F/GAS MARK 6

6 fresh spinach leaves
1 quantity Potato Base (see page 160)
1 quantity Special Tomato Sauce (see page 164)
1 tomato, sliced
1 celery stick, sliced thinly
½ green (bell) pepper, cored, deseeded and sliced thinly
1 baby courgette (zucchini), sliced
30 g/1 oz asparagus tips
30 g/1 oz sweetcorn, defrosted if frozen
30 g/1 oz peas, defrosted if frozen
4 spring onions (scallions), trimmed and chopped
1 tbsp chopped fresh mixed herbs, such as tarragon and parsley
60 g/2 oz Mozzarella cheese, grated
2 tbsp grated Parmesan cheese
1 artichoke heart
olive oil for drizzling
salt and pepper

1 Remove any stalks from the spinach and wash the leaves in plenty of cold water. Pat dry with paper towels.

2 Roll out or press the potato base, using a rolling pin or your hands, into a large 25 cm/10 inch circle on a lightly floured work surface (counter). Place the round on a large greased baking sheet (cookie sheet) or pizza pan and push up the edge a little to form a rim. Spread with the tomato sauce.

3 Arrange the spinach leaves on the sauce, followed by the tomato slices. Top with the remaining vegetables and herbs.

4 Mix together the cheeses and sprinkle over. Place the artichoke heart in the centre. Drizzle the pizza with a little olive oil and season.

5 Bake in a preheated oven for 18–20 minutes or until the edges are crisp and golden. Serve immediately.

SPINACH

Bags of young spinach leaves are available in most supermarkets. The spinach has been washed and the large stalks have been removed. Use the required amount of spinach on the pizza and use the remainder in a salad.

STEP 2

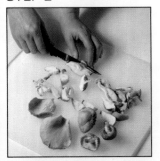

STEP 3

STEP 3

STEP 4

WILD MUSHROOM & WALNUT

Wild mushrooms make a delicious pizza topping when mixed with walnuts and Roquefort. If possible, use a mixture of oyster and shiitake mushrooms and ceps.

SERVES 2–4
OVEN: 200°C/400°F/GAS MARK 6

1 quantity Scone (Biscuit) Base (see
    page 158)
1 quantity Special Tomato Sauce (see
    page 164)
125 g/4 oz soft cheese
1 tbsp chopped fresh mixed herbs, such as
    parsley, oregano and basil
250 g/8 oz wild mushrooms, such as
    oyster, shiitake or ceps, or 125 g/4 oz
    each wild and button mushrooms
2 tbsp olive oil
1/4 tsp fennel seeds
30 g/1 oz walnuts, roughly chopped
45 g/1 1/2 oz Roquefort cheese
olive oil, to drizzle
salt and pepper
flat-leaf parsley sprig, to garnish

1 Roll out or press the scone (biscuit) base, using a rolling pin or your hands, into a 25 cm/10 inch circle on a lightly floured work surface (counter). Place on a large greased baking sheet (cookie sheet) or pizza pan and push up the edge a little with your fingers to form a rim.

2 Spread with the tomato sauce almost to the edge of the pizza base.

Dot with the soft cheese and herbs.

3 Wipe and slice the mushrooms. Heat the oil in a large frying pan (skillet) and stir-fry the mushrooms and fennel seeds for 2–3 minutes. Spread over the pizza with the walnuts.

4 Crumble the cheese over the pizza, drizzle with a little olive oil and season.

5 Bake in a preheated oven for 18–20 minutes or until the edge is crisp and golden. Serve immediately garnished with a sprig of flat-leaf parsley.

MUSHROOMS

Wild mushrooms each have their own distinctive flavours and make a change from button mushrooms. But they can be very expensive, so you can always use a mixture with chestnut (crimini) or button mushrooms instead.

GARLIC FLAVOUR

For added flavour, use a soft cheese with garlic and herbs.

ROASTED VEGETABLE & GOAT'S CHEESE

Wonderfully colourful vegetables are roasted in olive oil with thyme and garlic. The goat's cheese adds a nutty, piquant flavour.

STEP 1

SERVES 2–4
OVEN: 200°C/400°F/GAS MARK 6

2 baby courgettes (zucchini), halved
   lengthways
2 baby aubergines (eggplants), quartered
   lengthways
½ red (bell) pepper, cored, deseeded and cut
   into 4 strips
½ yellow (bell) pepper, cored, deseeded and
   cut into 4 strips
1 small red onion, cut into wedges
2 whole garlic cloves
4 tbsp olive oil
1 tbsp red wine vinegar
1 tbsp chopped fresh thyme
1 quantity Bread Dough Base (see
   page 156)
1 quantity Tomato Sauce (see page 163)
90 g/ 3 oz goat's cheese
salt and pepper
fresh basil leaves, to garnish

1 Place all the prepared vegetables in a large roasting tin (pan). Mix together the olive oil, vinegar, thyme and plenty of seasoning and pour over, coating all the vegetables well.

2 Bake in a preheated oven for 15–20 minutes until the skins on the vegetables have started to blacken in places. Turn the vegetables over half-way through cooking. Leave the vegetables to rest for 5 minutes after roasting.

3 Peel the roast (bell) peppers and the garlic cloves. Slice the garlic.

4 Roll out or press the dough, using a rolling pin or your hands, into a 25 cm/10 inch circle on a lightly floured work surface (counter). Place on a large greased baking sheet (cookie sheet) or pizza pan and raise the edge a little. Cover and leave for 10 minutes to rise slightly in a warm place. Spread with the tomato sauce almost to the edge.

5 Arrange the roasted vegetables on top and dot with the cheese. Drizzle the oil and juices from the roasting tin (pan) over the pizza and season.

6 Bake in a preheated oven for 18–20 minutes or until the edge is crisp and golden. Serve immediately, garnished with basil leaves.

STEP 2

STEP 3

STEP 5

STEP 1

STEP 2

STEP 3

STEP 4

TOFU (BEAN CURD) PIZZA

Chunks of tofu (bean curd) marinated in ginger and soy sauce impart something of an Oriental flavour to this pizza. The base is made from semolina, which gives it an unusual texture.

Serves 2–4
Oven: 200°C/400°F/Gas Mark 6

1 litre/1¾ pints/4 cups milk
1 tsp salt
250 g/8 oz semolina
1 tbsp soy sauce
1 tbsp dry sherry
½ tsp grated ginger root
285 g/9½ oz cake tofu (bean curd), cut into
    chunks
2 eggs
60 g/2 oz Parmesan cheese, grated
1 quantity Tomato Sauce (see page 163)
30 g/1 oz baby sweetcorn, quartered
30 g/1 oz mangetout (snow peas), trimmed
    and quartered
4 spring onions (scallions), trimmed and cut
    into 2.5 cm/1 inch strips
60 g/2 oz Mozzarella cheese, sliced thinly
2 tsp sesame oil
salt and pepper

1 Bring the milk to the boil with the salt. Sprinkle the semolina over the surface, stirring all the time. Cook for 10 minutes over a low heat, stirring occasionally, taking care not to let it burn. Remove from the heat and leave to cool until tepid.

2 Mix the soy sauce, sherry and ginger together in a bowl, add the tofu (bean curd) and stir gently to coat. Leave to marinate in a cool place for about 20 minutes.

3 Beat the eggs with a little pepper. Add to the semolina with the Parmesan and mix well. Place on a large greased baking sheet (cookie sheet) or in a pizza pan and pat into a 2.5 cm/ 10 inch round, using the back of a metal spoon or wetted hands. Spread with the tomato sauce almost to the edge.

4 Blanch the sweetcorn and mangetout (snow peas) for 1 minute, drain and place on the pizza with the drained tofu (bean curd). Top with the spring onions (scallions) and cheese. Drizzle over the sesame oil and season.

5 Bake in a preheated oven for 18–20 minutes or until the edge is crisp and golden. Serve immediately.

GINGER

Ginger root freezes well, so keep some in the freezer and just break off pieces when required.

CHAPTER THIRTEEN

Different Pizza Shapes

We usually think of a pizza as being round, but pizzas can be made in many shapes and sizes. Often they are made in a rectangle and cut into squares or strips to serve.

If you use alternative bases to the more traditional doughs, you will get a variety of different shapes depending on what you use. For instance, Italian bread pizzas are long, as the bases are made from an Italian loaf that has been halved lengthways. These make very good pizza bases, particularly as they are quick to prepare, and make perfect individual meals.

Pitta breads, muffins, rolls, baps and croissants can all be used for bases. As they have all been pre-baked, care must be taken not to overbake them, as this will result in a dried-out base. In some cases it might be preferable to cook the pizza under a grill (broiler) rather than in the oven, as this would cook the topping without drying out the base.

Opposite: *The Spanish Steps in the city of Rome, covered as always with a stunning floral display.*

199

STEP 1

STEP 2

STEP 3

STEP 4

PISSALADIERE

This is a traditional Mediterranean-style pizza, in which the main ingredient is onions. A lattice pattern is made with anchovies and black olives. This pizza is rectangular in shape and can be cut into squares or strips to serve.

MAKES 6 SQUARES
OVEN: 200°C/400°F/GAS MARK 6

4 tbsp olive oil
3 onions, sliced thinly
1 garlic clove, crushed
1 tsp soft brown sugar
½ tsp crushed fresh rosemary
220 g/7½ oz can chopped tomatoes
1 quantity Bread Dough Base (see page 156)
2 tbsp grated Parmesan cheese
60 g/2 oz can anchovies
12–14 black olives
salt and black pepper

1 Heat 3 tablespoons of the oil in a large saucepan and add the onions, garlic, sugar and rosemary. Cover the pan and fry gently for 10 minutes until the onions have softened but not browned, stirring occasionally. Add the tomatoes, stir and season well. Leave to cool slightly.

2 Roll out or press the dough, using a rolling pin or your hands, on a lightly floured work surface (counter) to fit a 30 × 18 cm/12 × 7 inch greased Swiss roll tin (jelly roll pan). Place in the tin (pan) and push up the edges slightly.

3 Brush the remaining oil over the dough and sprinkle with the cheese. Cover and leave to rise slightly in a warm place for about 10 minutes.

4 Spread the onion and tomato topping over the base. Remove the anchovies from the can, reserving the oil. Split each anchovy in half lengthways and arrange on the pizza in a lattice pattern. Place olives in between the anchovies and drizzle over a little of the reserved oil. Season.

5 Bake in a preheated oven for 18–20 minutes or until the edges are crisp and golden. Cut into squares and serve immediately.

PARTY PIZZA

For a great party pizza, make twice the size in a large greased roasting tin (pan), doubling up on the ingredients, and bake until the edges are golden.

STEP 1

STEP 2

STEP 3

STEP 5

PINEAPPLE MUFFINS

Halved toasted muffins are topped with pineapple and Parma ham (prosciutto), which is an Italian dry-cured ham. Plain, wholemeal (whole wheat) or cheese muffins all make great pizza bases.

SERVES 4
OVEN: 200°C/400°F/GAS MARK 6

4 muffins
1 quantity Tomato Sauce (see page 163)
2 sun-dried tomatoes in oil, drained and
  chopped
60 g/2 oz Parma ham (prosciutto)
2 rings canned pineapple, chopped
¹/₂ green (bell) pepper, cored, deseeded and
  chopped
125 g/4 oz Mozzarella cheese, sliced thinly
olive oil for drizzling
salt and pepper
small fresh basil leaves, to garnish

1 Cut the muffins in half and toast the cut side lightly.

2 Divide the sauce evenly between the muffins and spread over.

3 Sprinkle over the sun-dried tomatoes.

4 Cut the ham into thin strips and place on the muffins with the pineapple and green (bell) pepper.

5 Lay the Mozzarella slices on top of the pineapple and (bell) pepper.

6 Drizzle a little olive oil over the whole pizza and season.

7 Place under a preheated medium grill (broiler) and cook until the cheese melts and bubbles.

8 Serve immediately, garnished with small basil leaves.

MUFFINS

Muffins freeze well, so always keep some in the freezer for an instant pizza. To freeze muffins, put them into a plastic bag, seal and label the bag with the date and contents.

PREPARING PINEAPPLE

To prepare a fresh pineapple, slice off the skin from the top, bottom and sides. Remove the eyes with a sharp knife or the end of a potato peeler. Cut the pineapple into chunks. The pineapple will lose a lot of juice as you peel it – save as much as you can, and drink it later.

FRENCH BREAD PIZZAS

*Halved baguettes are a ready-made pizza base. The colours of the
tomatoes and cheese contrast beautifully on top. Try an onion or a
Granary baguette, or Italian ciabatta bread, which makes a really
good base.*

STEP 2

SERVES 4
OVEN: 200°C/400°F/GAS MARK 6

2 baguettes
1 quantity Tomato Sauce (see page 163)
4 plum tomatoes, sliced thinly lengthways
150 g/5 oz Mozzarella cheese, sliced thinly
10 black olives, cut into rings
8 fresh basil leaves, shredded
olive oil for drizzling
salt and pepper

1 Cut the baguettes in half
lengthways and toast the cut side
of the bread lightly.

2 Spread the toasted baguettes with
the tomato sauce.

3 Arrange the tomato and
Mozzarella slices alternately along
the length.

4 Top with the olive rings and half
the basil. Drizzle over a little olive
oil and season well.

5 Either place under a preheated
medium grill (broiler) and cook
until the cheese melts and is bubbling
or bake in a preheated oven at for 15–20
minutes.

6 Sprinkle over the remaining basil
and serve immediately.

STEP 3

STEP 4

DIFFERENT BREAD BASES

There are many different types of bread
available which would be suitable for
these pizzas. Italian ciabatta bread is made
with olive oil and is available both plain
and with different ingredients, such as
small pieces of black olives or sun-dried
tomatoes, mixed in.

INSTANT PIZZA

Make up double quantities and freeze half
of the pizzas. Reheat them from frozen in
the oven for about 15 minutes for an
instant snack.

STEP 6

STEP 2

STEP 3

STEP 4

STEP 5

CALZONE

A calzone is like a pizza in reverse – it resembles a large pasty with the dough on the outside and the filling on the inside. In Italian the word 'calzone' actually means trousers! If you are going on a picnic, take a calzone pizza as it can be eaten cold and is easy to transport.

SERVES 2–4
OVEN: 200°C/400°F/GAS MARK 6

1 quantity Bread Dough Base (see
   page 156)
1 egg, beaten
1 tomato
1 tbsp tomato purée (paste)
30 g/1 oz Italian salami, chopped
30 g/1 oz mortadella ham, chopped
30 g/1 oz Ricotta cheese
2 spring onions (scallions), trimmed and
   chopped
¼ tsp dried oregano
salt and pepper

1 Roll out the dough into a 23 cm/ 9 inch round on a lightly floured work surface (counter).

2 Brush the edge of the dough with a little beaten egg.

3 To skin the tomato, cut a cross in the skin and immerse it in boiling water for 45 seconds. Remove and rinse in cold water; the skin should slide off easily. Chop the tomato.

4 Spread the tomato purée (paste) over half the round nearest to you. Scatter the salami, mortadella and

chopped tomato on top. Dot with the Ricotta and sprinkle over the spring onions (scallions) and oregano. Season well.

5 Fold the other half of the dough towards you to form a half moon. Press the edges together well to prevent the filling from coming out.

6 Place on a baking sheet (cookie sheet) and brush with beaten egg to glaze. Make a hole in the top to allow steam to escape.

7 Bake in a preheated oven for 20 minutes or until golden.

VEGETARIAN VERSION

For a vegetarian calzone, replace the salami and mortadella with mushrooms or cooked chopped spinach.

STEP 1

STEP 4

STEP 6

STEP 7

RAISIN & (BELL) PEPPER

The vibrant colours of the (bell) peppers and onion make this a delightful pizza. Served cut into fingers, it is ideal for a party or buffet.

MAKES 8
OVEN: 200°C/400°F/GAS MARK 6

1 quantity Bread Dough Base (see
    page 156)
2 tbsp olive oil
½ each red, green and yellow (bell) pepper,
    cored, deseeded and sliced thinly
1 small red onion, sliced thinly
1 garlic clove, crushed
1 quantity Tomato Sauce (see page 163)
3 tbsp raisins
30 g/1 oz pine kernels (nuts)
1 tbsp chopped fresh thyme
olive oil for drizzling
salt and pepper

1 Roll out or press the dough, using a rolling pin or your hands, on a lightly floured work surface (counter) to fit a 30 × 18 cm/12 × 7 inch greased Swiss roll tin (jelly roll pan).

2 Place in the tin (pan) and push up the edges slightly.

3 Cover and leave to rise slightly in a warm place for about 10 minutes.

4 Heat the oil in a large frying pan (skillet). Add the (bell) peppers, onion and garlic and fry gently for 5

minutes until they have softened but not browned. Leave to cool.

5 Spread the tomato sauce over the base almost to the edge.

6 Sprinkle over the raisins and top with the cooled (bell) pepper mixture. Add the pine kernels (nuts) and thyme. Drizzle with a little olive oil and season well.

7 Bake in a preheated oven for 18–20 minutes or until the edges are crisp and golden. Cut into fingers and serve immediately.

RAISINS

Soak the raisins in some warm water for 15 minutes before adding them to the pizza, as this will keep them plump and moist when they are baked.

MINI PITTA BREAD CANAPES

Smoked salmon and asparagus make extra special party pizza canapés.
Mini pitta breads make great bases and are really quick.

STEP 1

STEP 3

STEP 5

STEP 6

MAKES 16
OVEN: 200°C/400°F/GAS MARK 6

8 thin asparagus spears
16 mini pitta breads
1 quantity Special Tomato Sauce (see
    page 164)
30 g/1 oz mild Cheddar cheese, grated
30 g/1 oz Ricotta cheese
60 g/2 oz smoked salmon
olive oil for drizzling
pepper

1 Cut the asparagus spears into 2.5 cm/1 inch lengths, then cut each piece in half lengthways.

2 Blanch the asparagus in boiling water for 1 minute. Drain and plunge into cold water.

3 Place the pitta breads on 2 baking sheets (cookie sheets). Spread about 1 teaspoon tomato sauce on each.

4 Mix the cheeses together and divide between the 16 pitta breads.

5 Cut the smoked salmon into 16 long thin strips. Arrange 1 strip on each pitta bread with the asparagus spears.

6 Drizzle over a little olive oil and season with pepper.

7 Bake in a preheated oven for 8–10 minutes. Serve immediately.

ECONOMY VERSIONS

Smoked salmon is expensive, so for a cheaper version, try using smoked trout. It is often half the price of smoked salmon, and tastes just as good. Try experimenting with other smoked fish, such as smoked mackerel, with its strong, distinctive flavour, for a bit of variety.

ASPARAGUS

Blanching the asparagus helps to soften it before topping the canapés. Plunge it into cold water after blanching, as this helps it to keep its colour.

CHAPTER FOURTEEN

Inventive Pizzas

In this chapter anything goes! Pizzas can be topped with almost any ingredient, so let your imagination go and make up your own individual recipes.

Pizza-making can be really fun for children. Let them create animal or funny faces from a range of ingredients such as vegetables, cheese and pasta. The results may help to encourage difficult eaters to clear their plates.

The Sunday morning fry-up will never be the same after trying a breakfast pizza – or even a corned beef hash pizza, which would be just as good for breakfast. Experiment with different flavours and you will be surprised by what you can come up with.

Opposite: *Rome's famous Trevi Fountain.*

STEP 1

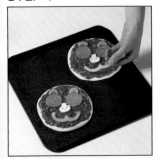

STEP 4

STEP 6

STEP 7

FUNNY FACES

These individual pizzas have faces made from sliced vegetables and spaghetti or noodles. Children love pizzas and will enjoy making their own. Use whatever suitable vegetables you have and let them have fun making all sorts of funny faces.

SERVES 4
OVEN: 200°C/400°F/GAS MARK 6

1 quantity Bread Dough Base (see
  page 156)
30 g/1 oz spaghetti or egg noodles
1 quantity Tomato Sauce (see page 163)
8 slices pepperoni-style sausage
8 thin sticks celery
4 slices button mushrooms
4 slices yellow (bell) pepper
4 slices Mozzarella cheese
4 slices courgette (zucchini)
olive oil for drizzling
8 peas

1 Divide the dough into 4 pieces. Roll each piece out into a 12 cm/5 inch circle and place on greased baking sheets (cookie sheets). Cover and leave to rise slightly in a warm place for about 10 minutes.

2 Cook the spaghetti or egg noodles according to the instructions printed on the packet.

3 Divide the tomato sauce evenly between each pizza base and spread out almost to the edge.

4 To make the faces, use pepperoni slices for the main part of the eyes, celery for the eyebrows, mushrooms for the noses and (bell) pepper slices for the mouths.

5 Cut the Mozzarella and courgette (zucchini) slices in half. Use the cheese for the cheeks and the courgettes (zucchini) for the ears.

6 Drizzle a little olive oil over each pizza and bake in a preheated oven for 12–15 minutes until the edges are crisp and golden.

7 Transfer the pizzas to serving plates and place the peas in the centre of the eyes. Drain the spaghetti or noodles and arrange around the tops of the pizzas for hair. Serve immediately.

CAT PIZZA

Make cat-face pizzas by using chicory (endive) for the ears, a mushroom for the nose and spaghetti for whiskers. Cut out cat-eye shapes from pepperoni or (bell) peppers, and add a pasta bow tie.

STEP 2

STEP 3

STEP 4

STEP 6

BREAKFAST

For a really substantial start to the morning, try a breakfast pizza! Sausages, bacon and mushrooms on a bread base topped with a fried egg will probably see you through the day.

SERVES 4
OVEN: 200°C/400°F/GAS MARK 6

1 quantity Bread Dough Base (see page 156)
12 skinless cocktail sausages
3 tbsp oil
1 quantity Tomato Sauce (see page 163)
150 g/5 oz can baked beans
4 rashers (slices) back bacon
60 g/2 oz baby button mushrooms, wiped and quartered
1 small tomato, cut into 8 wedges
60 g/2 oz Cheddar cheese, grated
4 eggs
salt and pepper

1 Roll out or press the dough, using a rolling pin or your hands, into a 25 cm/10 inch circle on a lightly floured work surface (counter). Place on a large greased baking sheet (cookie sheet) or pizza pan and push up the edge slightly to form a rim. Cover and leave to rise slightly for 10 minutes in a warm place.

2 Brown the cocktail sausages in a frying pan (skillet) with 1 tablespoon of the oil.

3 Mix the tomato sauce with the baked beans and spread over the base almost to the edge. Add the sausages on top.

4 Cut the bacon into strips and arrange on the pizza with the mushrooms and tomato. Sprinkle over the cheese and season.

5 Bake in a preheated oven for 18–20 minutes or until the edge is crisp and golden.

6 Add the remaining oil to the frying pan (skillet) and fry the eggs. When the pizza is cooked, cut into 4 pieces and top each with a fried egg. Serve immediately.

PLANNING AHEAD

To save time in the morning, you can make the tomato sauce and bread dough the night before. After the dough has been kneaded, wrap well and place in the refrigerator (if it is cold enough, this should prevent the dough from rising). After rolling out, the dough will take about 10 minutes longer to rise.

STEP 1

STEP 2

STEP 3

STEP 4

CORNED BEEF HASH

A combination of corned beef and baked eggs on a soured cream and potato base makes a really unusual pizza. Make sure each well is big enough to hold an egg before dropping it in!

SERVES 2–4
OVEN: 200°C/400°F/GAS MARK 6

500 g/1 lb potatoes
3 tbsp soured cream
325 g/11 oz can corned beef
1 small onion, finely chopped
1 green (bell) pepper, cored, deseeded and
    chopped
3 tbsp tomato and chilli relish
1 quantity Special Tomato Sauce (see
    page 164)
4 eggs
30 g/1 oz Mozzarella cheese, grated
30 g/1 oz Cheddar cheese, grated
paprika
salt and pepper
chopped fresh flat-leaf parsley, to garnish

1 Peel the potatoes and cut into even-sized chunks. Parboil them for 5 minutes in boiling salted water. Drain, rinse in cold water and cool.

2 Grate the potatoes and mix with the soured cream and seasoning in a bowl. Place on a large greased baking sheet (cookie sheet) or pizza pan and pat out into a 25 cm/10 inch round, pushing up the edge slightly to form a rim.

3 Mash the corned beef roughly with a fork and stir in the onion, green (bell) pepper and relish. Season well.

4 Spread the tomato sauce over the potato base almost to the edge. Top with the corned beef mixture. Using a spoon, make 4 wells in the corned beef. Break an egg into each.

5 Mix the cheeses together and sprinkle over the pizza with a little paprika. Season well.

6 Bake in a preheated oven for 20–25 minutes until the eggs have cooked but still have slightly runny yolks. Serve immediately garnished with chopped parsley.

ADDED EXTRAS

For extra colour, mix a grated carrot with the potato base. This will look and taste good, and will help to persuade your children to eat their vegetables, if they are fussy about that sort of thing. Use the tomato and chilli relish sparingly if you are serving this to children.

SPICY MEATBALL

Small minced (ground) beef meatballs, spiced with chillies and cumin seeds and covered in cheese and bacon, are baked on a scone (biscuit) base.

STEP 1

STEP 2

STEP 3

STEP 4

SERVES 2–4
OVEN: 200°C/400°F/GAS MARK 6

250 g/8 oz lean minced (ground) beef
30 g/1 oz jalapeño chillies in brine, chopped
1 tsp cumin seeds
1 tbsp chopped fresh flat-leaf parsley
1 tbsp beaten egg
3 tbsp olive oil
1 quantity Scone (Biscuit) Base (see page 158)
1 quantity Tomato Sauce (see page 163)
30 g/1 oz pimiento, sliced
2 slices streaky bacon, cut into strips
60 g/2 oz Cheddar cheese, grated
olive oil for drizzling
salt and pepper
chopped fresh flat-leaf parsley, to garnish

1 Mix the beef, chillies, cumin seeds, parsley and egg together in a bowl and season. Form into 12 small meatballs. Cover and chill for 1 hour.

2 Heat the oil in a large frying pan (skillet). Add the meatballs and brown all over. Remove with a perforated spoon or fish slice and drain on paper towels.

3 Roll out or press the dough, using a rolling pin or your hands, into a 25 cm/10 inch circle on a lightly floured work surface (counter). Place on a greased baking sheet (cookie sheet) or pizza pan and push up the edge slightly to form a rim.

4 Spread with the tomato sauce almost to the edge. Arrange the meatballs on the pizza with the pimiento and bacon. Sprinkle over the cheese and drizzle with a little olive oil. Season.

5 Bake in a preheated oven for 18–20 minutes or until the edge is golden and crisp.

6 Serve immediately garnished with chopped parsley.

MEATBALLS

If possible, make the meatballs in time to chill them for an hour before frying as this will help to stop them from breaking up during cooking.

STEP 1

STEP 3

STEP 5

STEP 8

AVOCADO & HAM

A smoked ham and avocado salad is served on a pizza with a base enriched with chopped sun-dried tomatoes and black olives, which are kneaded into the dough. If you are unable to buy Pipo Crème cheese, use blue Brie instead.

SERVES 2–4
OVEN: 200°C/400°F/GAS MARK 6

1 quantity Bread Dough Base (see
page 156)
4 sun-dried tomatoes, chopped
30 g/1 oz black olives, chopped
1 quantity Special Tomato Sauce (see
page 164)
4 small chicory (endive) leaves, shredded
4 small radicchio lettuce leaves, shredded
1 avocado, peeled, stoned (pitted) and sliced
60 g/2 oz wafer-thin smoked ham
60 g/2 oz Pipo Crème or other blue cheese,
cut into small pieces
olive oil for drizzling
salt and pepper
chopped fresh chervil, to garnish

1 Knead the dough gently, adding the sun-dried tomatoes and olives until mixed in.

2 Roll out or press the dough, using a rolling pin or your hands, into a 25 cm/10 inch circle on a lightly floured work surface (counter). Place on a greased baking sheet (cookie sheet) or pizza pan and push up the edge a little to form a rim.

3 Cover and leave to rise slightly in a warm place for 10 minutes before spreading with tomato sauce almost to the edge.

4 Top the pizza with shredded chicory (endive) and lettuce leaves and avocado slices.

5 Scrunch up the ham and add with the cheese.

6 Drizzle with a little olive oil and season well.

7 Bake in a preheated oven for 18–20 minutes or until the edge is crisp and golden.

8 Sprinkle with chervil to garnish and serve immediately.

HELPFUL HINTS

Before you use them, toss the avocado slices in a little fresh lemon juice to prevent the flesh from turning too brown. For a change, you could use wafer-thin smoked turkey instead of ham.

COMPLETE ITALIAN COOKING

Italian Cuisine

ITALIAN CUISINE

ITALIAN COOKING

Tourists flock in their millions to Italy, drawn by the ancient Roman architecture, the wealth of art galleries and churches, the Renaissance paintings and the famous, and now carefully restored, frescos by Michelangelo on the ceiling and walls of the Sistine Chapel in the Vatican, Rome. They also go to enjoy the warm, friendly atmosphere and the food!

A culinary history

The Italian cuisine that we know today is the result of a very chequered history. In the past, many different races invaded the Italian peninsula. The Etruscans brought polenta and the Greeks introduced wonderful seafood cookery. The Romans not only developed the Greek style of cookery but wrote down their recipes – and they still exist today.

Many peoples passed through Italy and brought in new ideas. In 1861, the Unification of Italy brought 20 separate regions together under one flag, but the different styles of cooking remained unchanged.

ITALIAN FOOD REGION BY REGION

There are two main culinary zones in Italy: the wine and olive zone, which lies around Umbria, Liguria and the South; and the cattle country, where the olive tree will not flourish – Emilia-Romagna, Lombardy and Veneto – but where milk and butter are widely produced. Tuscany, however, uses both butter and oil in its cooking because both cattle and olive trees flourish in the area.

Piedmont

The name means 'at the foot of the mountain', which it is, bordering on both France and Switzerland. Its fertile arable fields are irrigated by the many canals which flow through the region.

The food is substantial, peasant-type fare, though the fragrant white truffle is found in this region. Truffles can be finely flaked or grated and added to many of the smarter dishes, but they are wildly expensive. There is an abundance of wild mushrooms throughout the region. Garlic features strongly in the recipes and polenta, gnocchi and rice are eaten in larger quantities than pasta, the former being offered as a first course when soup is not served. A large variety of game is also widely available.

Lombardy

The mention of the capital, Milan, produces immediate thoughts of the wonderful risotto named after the city and also the Milanese soufflé flavoured strongly with lemon. Veal dishes, including *vitello tonnato* and *osso buco*, are specialities of the region and other excellent meat dishes, particularly pot roasts, feature widely.

The lakes of the area produce a wealth of fresh fish. Rice and polenta are again popular but pasta also appears in many guises. The famous sweet yeasted cake Panettone is a product of this region.

Trentino-Alto Adige

This is an area with a strong German influence, particularly when it comes to the wines. There are also several German-style liqueurs produced, such as Aquavit, Kümmel and Slivovitz.

The foods are robust and basic in this mountainous area with rich green valleys and lakes where fish are plentiful. In the Trentino area particularly, pasta and simple meat and offal dishes are popular, while in the Adige soups and pot roasts are favoured, often with added dumplings and spiced sausages.

Veneto

The cooking in this north-east corner is straightforward, with generous servings of polenta with almost everything. The land is intensively farmed, providing mostly cereals and wine. Pasta is less in evidence, with polenta, gnocchi and rice more favoured. Fish, particularly shellfish, is in abundance and especially good seafood salads are widely available. There are also excellent robust soups and risottos flavoured with the seafood and sausages of the area.

Liguria

The Genoese are excellent cooks, and all along the Italian Riviera can be found excellent trattoria which produce amazing fish dishes flavoured with the local olive oil. Pesto sauce flavoured with basil, cheese and pine kernels (nuts) comes from this area, along with other excellent sauces. The aroma of fresh herbs abounds, widely used in many dishes, including the famous pizzas.

Emilia-Romagna

This is a special region of high gastronomic importance, with an abundance of everything, and rich food is widely served. Tortellini and lasagne feature widely, along with many other pasta dishes, as do saltimbocca and other veal dishes. Parma is famous for its ham, *prosciutto di Parma*, thought to be the best in the world. Balsamic vinegar, which has grown in popularity over the past decade, is also produced here, from wine which is distilled until it is dark brown and extremely strongly flavoured.

Tuscany

The Tuscans share a great pride in cooking and eating with the Emilians, and are known to have hefty appetites. Tuscany has everything: an excellent coastal area providing splendid fish, hills covered in vineyards and fertile plains where every conceivable vegetable and fruit happily grows. There is plenty of game in the region, providing many interesting recipes; tripe cooked in a thick tomato sauce is popular along with many liver recipes; beans in many guises appear frequently, as well as pot roasts, steaks and full-bodied soups, all of which are well favoured.

Florence has a wide variety of specialities, while Siena boasts the famous candied fruit cake called Panforte di Siena.

Umbria/Marches

Inland Umbria is famous for its pork, and the character of the cuisine is marked by the use of the local fresh ingredients, including lamb, game and fish from the lakes, but is not spectacular on the whole. Spit-roasting and grilling is popular, and the excellent local olive oil is used both in cooking and to pour over dishes before serving. Black truffles, olives, fruit and herbs are plentiful and feature in many recipes. Eastwards to the Marches the wealth of fish from the coast adds even more to the variety and the food tends to be more on the elaborate side, with almost every restaurant noted for its excellent cuisine. First-class sausages and cured pork come from the Marches, particularly on the Umbrian border, and pasta features widely all over the region.

Lazio

Rome is the capital of both Lazio and Italy and thus has become a focal point for specialities from all over Italy. Food from this region tends to be fairly simple and quick to prepare, hence the many pasta dishes with delicious sauces, gnocchi in various forms and plenty of dishes featuring lamb and veal (saltimbocca being just one), and offal, all with plenty of herbs and seasonings giving really robust flavours and

The cooking of today

The most significant divide for Italy's cuisine is that between the industrial north and the poorer south. The north, with its fertile plains, its mountains and lakes, produces good-quality wines and dairy foods. By contrast, the sunnier, rockier south has olive groves, aubergines (eggplants), tomatoes and herbs. However, the regions do have features in common: the ingredients are fresh, techniques are simple, recipes are traditional and cooking, even in restaurants, is home-style.

BECHAMEL SAUCE

300 ml/½ pint/1¼ cups milk
2 bay leaves
3 cloves
1 small onion
60 g/2 oz/¼ cup butter, plus
    extra for greasing
45 g/1½ oz/6 tbsp flour
300 ml/½ pint/1¼ cups single
    cream
large pinch of grated nutmeg
salt and pepper

1. Pour the milk into a small pan and add the bay leaves. Press the cloves into the onion, add to the pan and bring the milk to the boil. Remove from the heat and set it aside to cool.

2. Strain the milk into a jug and rinse the pan. Melt the butter in the pan and stir in the flour. Stir for 1 minute, then gradually pour on the milk, stirring constantly. Cook the sauce for 3 minutes, then pour on the cream and bring it to the boil. Remove from the heat and season with nutmeg, salt and pepper.

CHEESE SAUCE

30 g/1 oz/2 tbsp butter
1 tbsp flour
250 ml/8 fl oz/1 cup milk
2 tbsp single cream
pinch of grated nutmeg
45 g/1½ oz Cheddar cheese,
    grated
1 tbsp grated Parmesan cheese

1. Melt the butter in a pan, stir in the flour and cook for 1 minute.

delicious sauces. Vegetables feature along with the fantastic fruits which are always in abundance in the local markets; and beans appear both in soups and many other dishes. The main theme of this region is strongly flavoured food with robust sauces.

Abruzzi and Molise

Formerly counted as just one region called Abruzzi e Molise, these regions have an interior of mountains with river valleys, high plateaux, densely forested areas and a coastal plain. The cuisine here is deeply traditional, with local hams and cheeses from the mountain areas, interesting sausages with plenty of garlic and other seasonings, cured meats, and wonderful fish and seafood, which is the main produce of the coastal areas, where fishing boats abound on the beaches. Lamb features widely: tender, juicy and well-flavoured with herbs.

Campania

Naples is the home of pasta dishes, served with a splendid tomato sauce (with many variations) famous worldwide. Pizza is said to have been created in Naples and now has spread to the north of the country and indeed all over the world.

Fish abounds, with *fritto misto* and *fritto pesce* being great favourites, varying daily depending on the catch. Fish stews are robust and varied and shellfish in particular is often served with pasta. Cutlets and steaks are excellent, served with strong sauces usually flavoured with garlic, tomatoes and herbs: pizzaiola steak is one of the favourites. Excellent Mozzarella cheese is produced locally and used to create the crispy Mozzarella in Carozza, again served with a garlicky tomato sauce. Sweet dishes are popular too, often with flaky pastry and Ricotta cheese, and the seasonal fruit salads laced with wine or liqueur take a lot of beating.

Puglia (Apulia)

The ground is stony but it produces good fruit, olive groves, vegetables and herbs, and, of course, there is a large amount of seafood from the sea. Puglians are said to be champion pasta eaters: many of the excellent pasta dishes are exclusive to the region both in shape and ingredients. Mushrooms abound and are always added to the local pizzas.

Oysters and mussels are plentiful, and so is octopus. Brindisi is famous for its shellfish – both the seafood salads and risottos are truly memorable. But it is not all fish or pasta: lamb is roasted and stewed to perfection and so is veal, always with plenty of herbs.

Basilicata

This is a sheep-farming area, mainly mountainous, where potent wines are produced to accompany a robust cuisine largely based on pasta, lamb, pork, game and abundant dairy produce. The salamis and cured meats are excellent, as are the mountain hams. Lamb is flavoured with the herbs and grasses on which it feeds. Wonderful thick soups – true minestrone – are produced in the mountains, and eels and fish are plentiful in the lakes. Chilli peppers are grown in this region and appear in many of the recipes. They are not overpoweringly strong, although the flavours of the region in general tend to be quite strong and intense. The cheeses are excellent, good fruit is grown and interesting local bread is baked in huge loaves.

Calabria

This is the toe of Italy, where orange and lemon groves flourish along with olive trees and a profusion of vegetables, especially aubergines (eggplants) which are cooked in a variety of ways.

Chicken, rabbit and guinea fowl are often on the menu. Pizzas feature largely, often with a fishy topping. Mushrooms grow well in the Calabrian climate and feature in many dishes from sauces and stews to salads. Pasta comes with a great variety of sauces including baby artichokes, eggs, meat, cheese, mixed vegetables, the large sweet (bell) peppers of the region and of course garlic. The fish is excellent too and fresh tuna and swordfish are available, along with many other varieties.

Like most southern Italians, the Calabrians are sweet-toothed and many desserts and cakes are flavoured with aniseed, honey and almonds and feature the plentiful figs of the region.

Sicily

This is the largest island in the Mediterranean and the cuisine is based mainly on fish and vegetables. Fish soups, stews and salads appear in unlimited forms, including tuna, swordfish, mussels and many more; citrus fruits are widely grown along with almonds and pistachio nuts, and the

local wines, including the dark, sweet, dessert wine Marsala, are excellent.

Meat is often given a long, slow cooking, or else is minced and shaped before cooking. Game is plentiful and is often cooked in sweet-sour sauces containing the local black olives.

Pasta abounds again with more unusual sauces as well as the old favourites. All Sicilians have a love of desserts, cakes and especially ice-cream. Cassata and other ice-creams from Sicily are famous all over the world, and the huge variety of flavours of both cream ices and granita makes it difficult to decide which is your favourite.

Sardinia

A pretty island with a wealth of flowers in the spring, but the landscape dries out in the summer from the hot sun. The national dish is suckling pig or newborn lamb cooked on an open fire or spit, and rabbit, game and offal dishes are also very popular.

The sweet dishes are numerous and often extremely delicate, and for non-sweet eaters there is fresh fruit of almost every kind in abundance.

Fish is top quality, with excellent sea bass, lobsters, tuna, mullet, eels and mussels in good supply.

The island has a haunting aroma which drifts from many kitchens – it is myrtle (*mirto*), a local herb which is added to anything and everything from chicken to the local liqueur; and along with the wonderful cakes and breads of Sardinia, myrtle will long remain a memory of the island when you have returned home.

2. Gradually pour on the milk, stirring all the time. Stir in the cream and season the sauce with nutmeg, salt and pepper.

3. Simmer the sauce for 5 minutes to reduce, then remove it from the heat and stir in the cheeses. Stir until the cheese has melted and blended into the sauce.

LAMB SAUCE

2 tbsp olive oil
1 large onion, sliced
2 celery sticks, thinly sliced
500 g/1 lb lean lamb, minced (ground)
3 tbsp tomato purée (paste)
150 g/5 oz bottled sun-dried tomatoes, drained and chopped
1 tsp dried oregano
1 tbsp red wine vinegar
150 ml/¹/₄ pint/²/₃ cup chicken stock
salt and pepper

1. Heat the oil in a frying pan over a medium heat and fry the onion and celery until the onion is translucent. Add the lamb and fry, stirring frequently, until it browns.

2. Stir in the tomato purée, sun-dried tomatoes, oregano, vinegar and stock. Season with salt and pepper.

3. Bring to the boil and cook, uncovered, for 20 minutes or until the meat has absorbed the stock. Taste and adjust the seasoning if necessary.

BASIC PASTA DOUGH

If you get caught up in the
enthusiasm of pasta making,
you might like to buy a
machine to roll, stretch and
cut the dough. However, once
it is fully and evenly stretched,
it is surprisingly easy to cut
by hand.

SERVES 4

*125 g/4 oz/1 cup strong plain
    (all-purpose) flour, plus extra
    for dusting
125 g/4 oz/⅔ cup fine semolina
1 tsp salt
2 tbsp olive oil
2 eggs
2–3 tbsp hot water*

1. Sieve the flour, semolina
and salt into a bowl and make
a well in the centre. Pour in
half the oil and add the eggs.
Add 1 tablespoon of hot water
and, using your fingertips,
work to a smooth dough.
Sprinkle on a little more water
if necessary to make the dough
pliable.

2. Lightly dust a board with
flour, turn the dough out and
knead it until it is elastic and
silky. This might take 10–12
minutes. Dust the dough with
more flour if your fingers
become sticky.

3. Alternatively, put the eggs,
1 tablespoon hot water and
the oil in the bowl of a food
processor and process for a
few seconds. Add the flour,
semolina and salt and process

GETTING TO KNOW PASTA

Pasta means 'paste' or 'dough' in Italian,
and many of the popular pasta dishes
have their origins in Italy, where it has
been produced since the thirteenth
century or earlier.

The principal ingredients of traditional
pasta are modest, although today there
are more types of fresh and dried pasta
available. By far the most popular type
is made from durum wheat, which is
milled to form fine semolina grains and
then extruded through drums fitted with
specially perforated discs, producing an
estimated 600 different pasta varieties.

Varieties of pasta

Pasta is made from either the endosperm
of the wheat, or from the whole wheat,
which contains more dietary fibre. Other
basic types are made from ground
buckwheat, which gives the product a
greyish colour and nutty flavour that
combines well with vegetable and herb
sauces; with the addition of spinach
paste, which produces an attractive
green colour – *lasagne verde* is a popular
example; and with a proportion of
tomato purée (paste), which produces a
deep coral colouring. *Pasta all'uovo*, made
with eggs, is produced in a range of flat
shapes, fresh or dried.

As well as green and red pasta, there
are other colours available: saffron pasta
is an attractive yellow-orange colour,
beetroot-hued pasta is a deep pink, and
pasta coloured with squid ink is a
dramatic black which makes any dish
truly eye-catching. You can also buy or
make pasta flecked with chopped basil
and other herbs.

Aside from these refinements of colour
and flavour, pasta is generally divided
into three main categories: long and
folded pasta, noodles and short pasta.

Since dried pasta has a shelf life of up to
6 months (see page 232) and fresh pasta
may be frozen for up to 6 months, it is a
good idea to build up your own selection
of varieties with which to surprise your
family and friends.

Pasta dictionary

The following is a glossary of some of the
most popular pasta shapes.

anelli and anellini small rings for soups

bozzoli deeply-ridged, cocoon-like shapes

bucatini long, medium-thick tubes

cappelletti wide-brimmed-hat shapes

cappelli d'angelo 'angel's hair', thinner
    than cappellini

cappellini fine strands of ribbon pasta

casareccia short curled lengths of pasta
    twisted at one end

cavatappi short, thick corkscrew shapes

conchiglie ridged shells

conchigliette little shells used in soup

cornetti ridged shells

cresti di gallo curved shapes

ditali, ditalini short tubes

eliche loose spiral shapes

elicoidali short, ridged tubes

farfalle bows

fedeli, fedelini fine tubes twisted into 'skeins'

festonati short lengths, like garlands

fettuccine ribbon pasta, narrower than tagliatelle

fiochette, fiochelli small bow shapes

frezine broad, flat ribbons

fusilli spindles, or short spirals

fusilli bucati thin spirals, like springs

gemelli 'twins', two pieces wrapped together

gramigna meaning 'grass' or 'weed'; the shapes look like sprouting seeds

lasagne flat, rectangular sheets

linguini long, flat ribbons

lumache smooth, snail-like shells popular with seafood sauces

lumachine U-shaped flat noodles

macaroni, maccheroni long or short-cut tubes, may be ridged or elbow-shaped

maltagliati triangular-shaped pieces, traditionally used in bean soups

noodles fine, medium or broad flat ribbons

orecchiette dished ear shapes

orzi tiny - like grains of rice, used in soups

pappardelle widest ribbons, either straight or sawtooth-edged

pearlini tiny discs

penne short, thick tubes with diagonal-cut ends

pipe rigate ridged, curved pipe shapes

rigatoni thick, ridged tubes

ruoti wheels

semini seed shapes

spaghetti fine, medium or thick rods

spirale two rods twisted into spirals

strozzapreti 'priest strangler', double twisted strands

tagliarini flat ribbon, thinner than tagliatelle

tagliatelle broad, flat ribbons

tortiglione thin, twisted tubes

vermicelli fine, slender strands usually sold folded into 'skeins'

ziti tagliati short, thick tubes

Nutritional value

Pasta has frequently had to answer to the charge that it is a fattening food which must be be avoided by anyone who is on a weight-reducing diet. The answer to that charge is that it may not be the pasta that piles on the calories, but more likely some of the sauces we choose to serve with it.

This table shows you some of the dietary and nutritional credentials of dry pasta.

	per 100g
Average moisture content	11.10
Protein	13.20
Fat	2.80
Dietary fibre (approx.)	10.00
Starch (as monosaccharide)	65.70
Calories	327.00

until smooth. Sprinkle on a little more hot water if necessary to make the dough pliable. Transfer to an electric mixer and knead using the dough hook for 2–3 minutes.

4. Divide the dough into 2 equal pieces. Cover a working surface (counter) with a clean cloth or tea towel (dish cloth) and dust it liberally with flour. Place one portion of the dough on the floured cloth and roll it out as thinly and evenly as possible, stretching the dough gently until the pattern of the weave shows through. Cover it with a cloth and roll out the second piece in a similar way.

5. Use a ruler and a sharp knife blade to cut long, thin strips for noodles, or small confectionery cutters to cut rounds, stars or other decorative shapes.

6. Cover the dough shapes with a clean cloth and leave them in a cool place (not the refrigerator) for 30–45 minutes to become partly dry, or place them in an airtight container for up to 24 hours.

7. Cook the fresh pasta in a large pan of boiling salted water, adding 1 tablespoon olive oil, for 3–4 minutes, until almost tender. Drain the pasta in a colander and serve with the sauce of your choice.

SPINACH & RICOTTA RAVIOLI

SERVES 4

1 recipe basic pasta dough (see
* pages 230-1)*
350 g/12 oz frozen spinach,
* thawed and chopped*
175 g/6 oz/³/₄ cup Ricotta cheese,
* or 90 g/3 oz each full-fat soft*
* cheese and cottage cheese*
4 tbsp grated Parmesan
salt and pepper
large pinch grated nutmeg

FOR THE SAUCE
25 g/1 oz/2 tbsp butter
150 ml/¹/₄ pint/²/₃ cup crème
* fraîche*
grated nutmeg

1. Turn the chopped spinach
into a colander and use a
wooden spoon to press out as
much of the liquid as possible.

2. Mix together the spinach and
cheeses and season the mixture
with salt, pepper and nutmeg.
(For a smooth filling, you can
mix the ingredients in a food
processor.)

3. Divide the dough into 2 equal
pieces and roll out each one as
described on page 231Cut one
sheet into strips about
7.5cm/3inches wide. Place
small heaps of the filling at
7.5 cm/3 inch intervals close to
one side of each strip. Fold the
strips over, press the edges to
seal them and repeat with the
remainder of the dough. Cut out
the ravioli squares. A pastry
wheel is useful for this, as it
helps to seal the joins as it cuts.

COOKING PASTA

The real enjoyment of pasta depends
upon the cooking; undercooked, and it
will be unyielding and taste of raw flour;
overcooked, and it will be soft and stick.
The Italians describe the perfect texture
as *al dente*, meaning that the pasta is still
slightly resistant to the bite.

Cooking times vary according to the
type and volume of the pasta, and you
should always follow those recommended
on the packet. In general, fresh pasta will
be cooked in 3–5 minutes. dried pasta in
around 6 minutes for fine strands such as
vermicelli; 7–12 minutes for quick-
cooking macaroni, spaghetti and noodles;
and 10–15 minutes for cannelloni tubes
and sheets of lasagne.

Whatever the pasta type, have ready a
pan of water at a steady, rolling boil. Add
salt, and 1 tablespoon of olive oil, to
prevent sticking. Add the pasta gradually,
a handful or a few strands at a time so
that the water continues to boil and the
pasta is kept separate. Do not completely
cover the pan, or the water will boil over.
Leave it uncovered, or partly covered.
Drain the cooked pasta into a colander
and, if it is not to be served at once, return
it to the pan with a little olive oil.

How much to allow

It is not possible to say exactly how much
pasta to allow for each person. It is worth
remembering that dried pasta more than
doubles in volume during cooking,
absorbing water until it is rehydrated. It
is usual to allow 40–50 g/1–2 oz dried
pasta per person for a first course or a
salad, and 75–100 g/3–4 oz dried pasta
for a main dish.

Storing and freezing pasta

Dried pasta will keep in good condition for
up to six months. Keep it in the packet,
and reseal it once you have opened it, or
transfer the pasta to an airtight jar.

Fresh pasta has a very short storage life,
only one or two days in the refrigerator,
so buy it only when you want to serve it.

Cooked pasta may be stored for up to
three days in the refrigerator. If the pieces
have stuck together, turn them in a
colander and run warm water through
them. Drain well, then toss the pasta in
hot olive oil or melted butter before
serving.

It is possible to freeze cooked pasta for
up to 3 months. But it must be thawed at
room temperature before reheating.

PASTA MACHINES

Pasta machines that will stretch and roll
the dough are widely available. You will
also need plenty of space for the rolled-out
dough, as well as somewhere to hang the
dough to dry.

The method is to feed the pasta through
the rollers repeatedly one notch thinner
each time. This is time-consuming but
important, as the pasta needs to keep its
elasticity.

To roll the pasta from the recipe on page
230-1, first divide the dough into 2 pieces.
If the pasta strip becomes too long and
unwieldy as it stretches, cut it again. Roll
until all the pieces have gone through the
machine at each setting. Lay the pasta out
on tea towels to dry until it feels leathery
which is when it is ready to be cut. The
machine will cut pasta into strips for
ribbon pasta; other shapes will have to be
cut by hand. To use the pasta strips

immediately, place a tea towel over the back of a chair and hang the strips to dry.

PASTA SAUCES

Creative cooks will enjoy partnering their favourite sauces with a variety of pastas. Although there are classic combinations such as Spaghetti Bolognese and Spaghetti Carbonara, there are no rules, just guidelines. Guidelines which are largely a matter of practicality, appearance and taste. For example, use pasta shells to evoke the appropriate image and texture when eating with fish and shell-fish sauces.

Cheeses with pasta

Some cheeses have a natural affinity with pasta dishes and appear frequently in recipes.

Ricotta A milky white, soft and crumbly Italian cheese which resembles cottage cheese. It is low in fat, being made from whey, but some varieties produced now have whole milk added. If you cannot obtain Ricotta, use another low-fat soft cheese. To obtain a smooth-textured sauce or filling press the substitute through a sieve.

Parmesan A mature and exceptionally hard cheese produced in Italy, Parmesan is the most important of flavourings for pasta. It may be useful to have a small carton of ready-grated Parmesan in the refrigerator, but you will find that it quickly loses its pungency and 'bite'. For that reason, it is better to buy small quantities of the cheese in one piece and grate it yourself. Tightly wrapped in clingfilm and foil, it can be kept in the refrigerator for several months. Grate it just before serving, for maximum flavour.

Pecorino A hard sheep's milk cheese which resembles Parmesan and is often used for grating over dishes. It has a sharp flavour and is only used in small quantities.

Mozzarella Another highly popular cheese, this is a soft cheese, with a piquant flavour, traditionally made from water buffalo's milk. Buffalo milk is now scarce, and so this cheese is often made with cow's milk. It can be used fresh, most popularly in salads, and also provides a tangy layer in baked dishes.

OLIVE OIL

Olive oil, which is at the heart of so many pasta dishes, has a personality all of its own, and each variety has its own characteristic flavour.

Extra-virgin olive oil This is the finest grade, made from the first, cold pressing of hand gathered olives. Always use extra-virgin oil for salad dressings.

Virgin olive oil This oil has a fine aroma and colour, and is also made by cold pressing. It may have a slightly higher acidity level than extra-virgin oil.

Refined or 'pure' olive oil This is made by treating the paste residue from the pressings with heat or solvents to remove the residual oil.

Olive oil is a blend of refined and virgin olive oil.

4. Cook the ravioli in a large pan of boiling water, to which you have added salt and 1 tablespoon olive oil, for 3–4 minutes.

5. Heat together the butter and crème fraîche and season with salt, pepper and nutmeg.

6. Drain the pasta in a colander, turn it into a warmed serving dish and pour over the sauce. Toss the ravioli to coat it thoroughly.

TOMATO SAUCE

2 tbsp olive oil
1 small onion, chopped
1 garlic clove, chopped
424 g / 15 oz can chopped
   tomatoes
2 tbsp chopped parsley
1 tsp dried oregano
2 bay leaves
2 tbsp tomato purée (paste)
1 tsp sugar

1. To make the tomato sauce, heat the oil in a pan over a medium heat and fry the onion until it is translucent. Add the garlic and fry for 1 further minute.

2. Stir in the chopped tomatoes, parsley, oregano, bay leaves, tomato purée (paste) and sugar and bring the sauce to the boil.

3. Simmer, uncovered, until the sauce has reduced by half, about 15–20 minutes. Taste the sauce and adjust the seasoning if necessary. Discard the bay leaves.

Pizza bases and their ingredients

Buy fresh yeast in bulk and freeze in 15g/½ oz quantities ready to use whenever needed.

To give the base extra flavour and a different texture, try adding to the flour fresh or dried herbs, chopped nuts or seeds, such as poppy, sunflower and sesame.

Always use a good olive oil such as extra virgin for the best flavour.

If time is short, place the bread dough in a food processor to knead for a few minutes.

If you have made the bread dough or scone (biscuit) base too wet, add a little extra flour and work it in. If the base is too dry, add a little extra water or milk in the same way.

Bread dough bases can be kept for several days before being used. After kneading, carefully wrap in clingfilm (plastic wrap) to prevent them from drying out in the refrigerator. Allow extra time for the dough to rise, as it will take a while for the dough to warm up and for the yeast to begin to work. If the dough is left uncovered and develops a crust, cover it with a damp cloth and the crust will soon disappear.

MAKING PIZZAS

The pizza has become a universally popular food, in every form from the genuine article – thin, crisp and oven-baked – to frozen and fast-food pizza slices. The delightful aroma of freshly baked bread topped with tomatoes, fresh herbs and cheese rarely fails to have a mouthwatering effect.

As well as being economical and popular, few other dishes are as versatile as the pizza, thanks to the countless possible permutations of bases and toppings that can be served to suit every palate and every occasion.

History of the pizza

Although there is much speculation about where pizza in its simplest form was first invented, it is usually associated with the old Italian city of Naples. It was then a simple street food, richly flavoured and quickly made. It was not always round and flat as we know it today, but was originally folded up like a book, with the filling inside, and eaten by hand. Pizzas were usually sold on the streets by street criers who carried them around in copper cylindrical drums kept hot by coals from the pizza ovens.

The word 'pizza' actually means any kind of pie. The classic Napoletana pizza is probably the best-known of the many varieties. This consists of a thin crust of dough topped simply with a fresh tomato sauce, Mozzarella cheese, olives, anchovies and a sprinkling of oregano. When baked, the flavours blend perfectly together to give the distinctive aromatic pizza. Another classic is the 'Margherita' pizza, named after the Italian Queen Margherita. Bored with their usual cuisine when on a visit to Naples, she asked to sample a local speciality. The local 'Pizzaiolo' created a pizza in the colours of the Italian flag – red tomatoes, green basil and white Mozzarella. The Queen was delighted, and it became widely celebrated.

BASIC PIZZA INGREDIENTS

Pizzas are made from very basic ingredients and are very simple to cook. Although making your own base and topping can be a little time-consuming, it is very straightforward, and you end up with a delicious home-baked dish, as well as a sense of achievement.

Flour

Traditional pizza bases are made from bread dough, which is usually made with strong plain bread flour. However, for the best results use ordinary plain flour. A strong flour will make the dough very difficult to stretch into whatever shape you choose to make your pizza.

For a brown bread base, use one of the many types of wholemeal (whole wheat) flours available on the market, such as stoneground wholemeal (whole wheat), wheatmeal and granary. Wheatgerm or bran can also be added to white flour for extra flavour, fibre and interest. Or you could mix equal quantities of wholemeal (whole wheat) and white flour.

Always sift the flour first, as this will remove any lumps and help to incorporate air in the flour, which will in turn help to produce a light dough. If you sift wholemeal (whole wheat) flours, there will be some bran and other bits left in the sieve, which are normally tipped back so that their goodness and fibre are added to the sifted flour.

Yeast thrives in warm surroundings, so all the ingredients for the bread dough base should be warm, as should the equipment used. If the tepid yeast liquid is added to a cold bowl containing cold flour, it will quickly cool down. This will retard the growth of the yeast, and the dough will take much longer to rise. If the flour is kept in a cool cupboard or larder, remember to get it out in plenty of time to allow it to warm to room temperature before you use it. Sift the flour into a large mixing bowl, then place it somewhere warm, such as an airing cupboard or even in a top oven on the lowest setting. Do not allow it to overheat, as this will kill the yeast.

Salt

Add the required amount of salt to the flour when sifting, as this will help to distribute it evenly throughout the resulting mixture. Salt is important, as it helps to develop the gluten in the flour. Gluten is the protein which produces the characteristic elasticity of the dough, but mostly it provides the dough with its flavour.

Yeast

There are three types of yeast available: fresh, dried and easy-blend. Fresh is usually found in health-food shops and is not expensive. Dissolve 15g/½ oz fresh yeast in 90ml/3½ fl oz tepid water with 2.5ml/½ tsp sugar and allow it to froth before adding it to the flour – about 5 minutes. The frothiness indicates that the yeast is working. Fresh yeast will keep for 4 to 5 days in the refrigerator. Make sure it is well covered, as it will dry out very quickly.

Dried yeast can be found in sachets or drums in most supermarkets and chemists. It has a shelf life of about 6 months, so buy only a small drum if you are not going to make bread dough on a regular basis. It is easy to make up a dough that won't rise, only to find out too late that the yeast has passed the sell-by date. Like fresh yeast, add it to the tepid water with a little sugar, and stir to dissolve. Allow the mixture to stand for 10–15 minutes until froth develops on the surface.

Easy-blend yeast is the simplest to use, as it is simply stirred dry into the flour before the water is added. It is available in sachet form and can be found in most supermarkets.

Water

It has been said that Naples produces the best pizzas because of the quality of its water! But as that may be a bit far to travel just to make a pizza, your local water will have to suffice. The water must be tepid, as this is the optimum temperature for the yeast to grow. Take care to add just the right amount of water stated in the recipe. If you add too much water, the dough will be difficult to handle and the cooked base will be too hard.

Kneading

This can be the most daunting procedure in bread-making, but it is a very necessary one. The best way of doing it is

Fillings and toppings

Avoid using starchy topping ingredients, as the base is very substantial and you will end up with a heavy pizza.

Make sure that you season the tomato sauce well, as this is the basis of the pizza, and a bland sauce will make for a bland pizza. Using a bay leaf makes a considerable difference – but don't forget to take it out!

Do not overfill a pizza, as it will overflow in the oven and will be difficult to eat.

Make a rim around the edge of the dough, as this will help to keep the topping on.

When making pizza for several people with differing tastes, place different toppings on separate sections of the pizza, or make individual ones in a selection of flavours. They can all cook at the same time, making it easy to suit all tastes.

To make pizza easier to handle, put the heavier topping ingredients near the edge of the pizza rather than in the middle. This will help to prevent it from sagging at the point when cut into wedges.

Drain all the pizza ingredients as much as possible before they are used. If you use spinach, squeeze out as much water as possible, or you will end up with a soggy pizza.

Grease the pizza pan or baking sheet well, to prevent the pizza from sticking.

Serving

Always serve a pizza as soon as it leaves the oven, as the cheese will set slightly and lose its elasticity as it cools down.

Place the pizza on a warmed serving plate when it comes out of the oven, to prevent it from going cold too quickly. Use a couple of large fish slices to transfer the pizza from the baking sheet or pizza pan to the serving plate.

Pizzas make excellent party food. Make them in large rectangles and cut into squares to serve.

Leftovers

Any leftover Mozzarella cheese can be grated and frozen, ready for the next time you want to make a pizza.

Leftover tomato sauce can be used up by adding it to casseroles, soups, and pasta dish sauces such as spaghetti and lasagne.

Accompaniments

Follow a pizza meal with a refreshing dessert, such as fresh fruit salad, sorbet or ice cream. Zabaglione, a light Italian dessert of eggs, sugar and Marsala wine, makes a perfect ending.

to take the edge of the dough that is furthest away from you and pull it into the centre towards you, then push it down with the heel of your hand, turning the dough round with your other hand as you go. The kneading process mixes all the ingredients together and strengthens the gluten, which holds the bubbles of air created by the yeast, which in turn causes the dough to rise. The dough must be kneaded for at least 5 minutes or until it becomes smooth and pliable and is no longer sticky.

Try adding extra ingredients to the dough when kneading, such as chopped sun-dried tomatoes or olives, to create a more interesting base.

The tomato sauce

Every pizza must have tomato sauce of some kind as the basis of the topping. This can be made using either canned or fresh tomatoes. There are many types of canned tomato available – for example, plum tomatoes, or tomatoes chopped in water, or chopped sieved tomato (passata). The chopped variety are often canned with added flavours such as garlic, basil, onion, chilli and mixed herbs, which will add more interest to your sauce. Make sure the sauce is well seasoned before adding it to your base, as a tasteless sauce will spoil your pizza.

Cheese

The cheese most often associated with the pizza is, of course, Mozzarella. It is a mild, white, delicate cheese traditionally made from buffalo milk. The best feature of this cheese as far as pizzas are concerned is its ability to melt and produce strings of cheese when a slice is cut and pulled away. It is sold in supermarkets, wrapped in small bags of whey to keep it moist. Slice, grate or cut it into small pieces before placing it on the pizza. Many supermarkets stock bags of pre-grated Mozzarella cheese, which is a great timesaver.

The other cheeses most often found on pizzas are Parmesan and Cheddar. The recipes in this book use a variety of different cheeses. If you are using strongly flavoured topping ingredients such as anchovies and olives, a milder-tasting cheese may be more suitable. Experiment with different cheeses to suit your taste.

TOPPING INGREDIENTS

There are a number of classic ingredients that are used regularly in pizza toppings, such as olives, anchovies, capers, mushrooms, (bell) peppers, artichokes and chillies, but most ingredients are suitable, if used in complementary combinations.

Be adventurous and experiment, but don't be afraid to stick to simple combinations of just two or three ingredients – often the simplest pizzas are the most delicious and the most memorable, as the flavours don't fight each other.

Herbs

Whenever possible, use fresh herbs. They are becoming more readily available, especially since the introduction of 'growing' herbs, small pots of herbs which you buy from the supermarket or greengrocer and grow at home. This not only ensures the herbs are as fresh as possible, but also provides a continuous supply.

If you use dried herbs, remember that you need only about one third of dried to fresh. The most popular pizza herbs are basil, oregano and parsley, although you can experiment with your favourite ones. Torn leaves of fresh basil on a tomato base is a simple but deliciously aromatic combination.

Baking
Traditionally pizzas are cooked in special ovens on a stone hearth. A large peel or paddle is used to slide them in and out. But at home it is best to place the dough on a baking sheet or in a pizza pan. The dough will expand while cooking, so make sure the baking sheet is big enough. Always push up the edge of the dough to form a rim to prevent the topping from spilling over while it cooks.

Time-savers
Fortunately for the busy cook, pizzas are an easy food to package and chill or freeze, ready to be cooked on demand. There is a wide range of ready-made pizza bases. Some come in packet form and only need to be mixed and shaped before they are ready for a topping, which can also be bought separately, most often in jars.

Pizzas are also sold complete with a variety of toppings, which you can bake as they are, or add more toppings yourself. Although they never seem to taste as good as a real homemade pizza, they can be very useful to keep on hand. Jars of peppers, sun-dried tomatoes and

artichokes in olive oil make very good toppings, and will keep for quite a while in your larder.

Serving
Pizzas should be served as soon as they leave the oven. Cut the pizza into wedges or strips using a sharp knife or pizza cutter. As pizza slices are easy to eat by hand, they make great party food.

Crisp salads, coleslaw and garlic bread go well with pizzas and help to make a balanced meal. Due to their rich flavour pizzas are best served with a well-chilled Italian table wine such as Frascati, Valpolicella or Chianti. If you are not a wine drinker, beer will go with pizza just as well.

Freezing
Pizzas are ideal standby food, as you can make and freeze them in advance, and both the bread dough and the complete pizza can be frozen. Make up double quantities of dough and freeze the half that is unused after it has been kneaded. Wrap in clingfilm (plastic wrap) and place in a freezer bag. Defrost at room temperature and allow to rise as normal. Alternatively, rise and roll out the dough, top with tomato sauce, cheese and any other topping ingredients and bake for only 10 minutes. Cool, wrap in a polythene bag and place in the freezer. Cook straight from the freezer in a hot oven for about 15 minutes.

The tomato sauce will keep well in a screw-topped jar in the refrigerator for up to a week, or can be placed in freezer-proof containers and frozen if you need to keep it for longer periods.

Garlic bread
Garlic bread is often served with pizza. Mix 1–2 cloves of crushed garlic with 125g/4 oz butter and spread it in between diagonal cuts made in a French bread stick. Wrap in foil and place in the bottom of the oven for 5 or 6 minutes while the pizza is cooking.

For herb bread, add chopped fresh parsley and chives to the butter before spreading it on the bread.

Salads
Salad-making has never been so simple, thanks to the bags of prepared salads available in most supermarkets. Choose a selection of unusual and exotic salad leaves to add colour and crunch to your salad. Chicory (endive), radiccio, oakleaf, curly endive, sorrel and lamb's lettuce all make an interesting change from the lettuce we are used to seeing in salads.

Use plenty of colour – red and yellow (bell) peppers, green mangetout (snow peas), cherry tomatoes and baby corn cobs are all readily available.

Make up your own dressing with 3 tbsp olive oil, 1 tbsp wholegrain mustard, 1 tbsp fresh chopped herbs and plenty of salt and pepper. Place in a screw-topped jar and shake well to blend. Pour over the prepared salad and toss well to mix. Add the dressing just before serving, or the lettuce leaves will wilt and go soggy.

INDEX